My Heart Is a Glowing Sunset
My Voice Is a Warming Song

My Heart Is a Glowing Sunset My Voice Is a Warming Song

*Selected Works From the COMPAS
Writers & Artists-in-the-Schools Program*

Edited by
Roy McBride

Illustrations by
William Jeter

COMPAS
Writers & Artists-in-the-Schools
1990

Publication of this book is generously supported by the Sven and C. Emil Berglund Foundation, dedicated in memory of C. Emil Berglund.

COMPAS programs are made possible in part by grants provided by the Minnesota State Arts Board, through an appropriation by the Minnesota State Legislature. The Minnesota State Arts Board received additional funds to support this activity from the National Endowment for the Arts. COMPAS is the recipient of a McKnight Foundation Award administered by the Minnesota State Arts Board, and is an affiliate of United Arts. In the past year, the COMPAS Writers & Artists-in-the-Schools program has received generous support from the Hugh J. Andersen Foundation, the Ashland Oil Foundation, the Cargill Foundation, Land O'Lakes and U S WEST Communications.

As always, we are grateful for the hundreds of excellent teachers throughout Minnesota who sponsor COMPAS Writers & Artists-in-the-Schools residencies. Without their support and hard work, the writers and artists would not weave their magic, and the student work we celebrate in this book would not spring to life.

ISBN 0-927663-15-5

COMPAS
305 Landmark Center
75 West Fifth Street
St. Paul, Minnesota 55102

Molly LaBerge, Executive Director
Daniel Gabriel, Director, Writers & Artists-in-the-Schools

Table of Contents

II. TIME CAPSULE

III. LOVE WILL BUILD A WALL

IV. My Name's Rescue

V. Symbol of Hope

INTRODUCTION

Listen.
Listen to the voices.
Listen to the voices of the children.
Listen to the voices of the children of Minnesota.
Listen.
Listen to their dreams.
Listen to their nightmares.
Listen to their feelings.
Listen to their concerns.
Listen to what they have to say about our relationships.
Listen to what they have to say about our world.
Listen.
Listen to the voices.
Listen to the voices of our children.

* * * * * * * * * * * *

POETS-IN-THE-SCHOOLS
    became
WRITERS-IN-THE-SCHOOLS
    became
WRITERS & ARTISTS-IN-THE-SCHOOLS
   (one day a couple years ago at a school
   in St. Paul I met a PHILOSOPHER-IN-THE-SCHOOLS)
   and we will become
               evolving
as the world is revolving
                  as we must evolve

keeps evolving
                    revolving

                * * * * * * * * * * *

Listen.
Word.
Imagination.
Words.
Imagination.
In our image — our words — our nation.
State of the word.
State of the imagination.
Stating our image of our nation.
Word.
Words.
Listen.

WRITERS IN THE SCHOOL

We remember you.
We remember schools.
We remember classes.
We remember students, teachers and support staff.
We remember.
We remember voices
                    and
                        words
                feelings so strong
                    imaginations so wild
                        we can never forget.
We remember.
We remember you.

                * * * * * * * * * * *

COMPAS

North

West   East

South

from and to
through
you and me
we
circle

listen
listen to the voices.

Roy McBride
August, 1990

Song of the Wind and Rain

MILKY WAY

The Milky Way's house is like a dark sky and for lights
little stars. The walls are made of thunder and the
heater is the sun and the windows are made of hail.
The rug is made of clouds. He has a treasure chest
full of diamonds. When there's an earthquake, he
takes a diamond and drops it in the earthquake and
it grows and it fills the earthquake.

Brandon Meyer :: Grade 3
North Elementary School :: St. Peter

Fall

> Fall is a giant losing
> his hair. When his hair falls,
> he blows it across the land.

Cloudy Days

> The clouds moving are
> the puffs of smoke from
> his pipe.

Cold Winters

> The mountains are lumps
> on his head from his wife
> Mars hitting him on the
> head with comets.

Spring

> Summer is when great great
> grandfather the sun comes to visit.

Rainy Days

> Rainy days are when Earth starts to
> cry for his supper.

Kyle Halvorson :: Grade 6
Viking Elementary School :: Newfolden

Northern Lights

Like natural Christmas lights
in the black night or a jet
of light in the sky like
a shield of light stirring
the darkness or like a search light
looking for the invisible
plane and that's what these
mystic mysterious lights are

Danny Barr :: Grade 5
Elm Creek Elementary School :: Maple Grove

Song of the Wind and the Rain

I am the wind,
playing a tune through the trees'
bare and empty branches.

I am a raindrop,
bringing relief to thirsty plants,
playing drums on a tin roof,
running down a dusty rock,
making it look like a zebra.

Go away blizzard,
You howl and shriek,
And make terrible noises.

You bring freezing weather,
And a silent cold.

You strip the leaves off the trees,
And tear the grass out of the ground.

You cover up needed food,
And life-saving shelters,
You blow your snow around and around,
Confusing and losing people and animals.

Ha, now you go!
No longer shall you hide the sun.

Jenny Fiedler :: Grade 6
St. Francis Xavier School :: Buffalo

Untitled

My friends, never go near
the place where sleet lives.
She will hurl herself down at you
and then take you to her home. She
is rude and obnoxious, mean and only
thinks of herself. She follows rain and
snow and they all have a party together.
When she gets bored, she will take
her army of freezing rain and snow and
they will drive off together on their herd
of clouds. They pick a town and hurl
themselves on the animals and people down below.
When Mr. Sun comes as the policeman
he will take Miss Sleet and melt
her army, but she will escape to a pole
and will be back for a rematch.

Anje Scholl :: Grade 5
West Elementary :: Worthington

RAIN

Rain chases pebbles and sand.
Rain makes soggy rabbit food,
thawing rainbows, and lightning look like
dotted streaks. Rain
sounds like a kid is beating on drums,
sizzling safari bacon and
frying potatoes.
Rain jumps over rocks, barks at stones,
fills chopped up soggy apples, bakes
on grass, and smells like roses.

Leticia Wessel :: Grade 5
Swanville Public School :: Swanville

Explain the Star at Dusk

The time of day is at dusk, who
says he saw the star. Explain
the thick fog covering the micro-
scopic star who glides through
the air like a fairy on her wand.
Who looks down deep at the
shining sea, with giant crows
yelling at him at once. Then . . .
a huge echo throughout the sky. The star
bursts. No need to explain the
foggy night at dusk!

Lindsay Murphy :: Grade 6
Tanglen Elementary School :: Minnetonka

SUNDAY SILENCE

Monday is a loud beginning —
people clamber out of bed
not to be late.

Tuesday and Wednesday go smoothly
slowly dampering
like the sound of a kettle drum dissolving.

But as Thursday approaches,
the tension increases and the melody changes.
As Friday comes near,
the earth vibrates.

Saturday is relaxed with a mellow tone
and familiar tempo.

On Sunday, there is a silence
that touches your soul
and forms the dark in a rainbow.

As Monday reappears,
you can hear the silence
breaking into a million pieces.

Tracy Winjun :: Grade 8
Caledonia Junior High School :: Caledonia

THAT NIGHT

the smell of fresh cut grass
ascends from the ground
my day pushing the mower is complete
my accomplishment vanished
covered in pure darkness till morning
warm air spreads fumes of
melted sunscreen
the aroma of fresh dew provides cool trickling air
like a silent slow waterfall
covering the earth with
tiny tears

Char Van Valkenburg :: Grade 11
Long Prairie High School :: Long Prairie

Untitled

My brother and I love the windy days.
Green foliage closing in around us.
My blond hair
blows swiftly in the wind.
Standing with trimming shears
on my right hip.
My brother pretends the sticks
on his head are deer antlers.
I, in my red pants
blue shirt,
white shoes,
and flowing blond hair
run on the hill with the wind
mad and furious
flowing against us like we're enemies
trying to stop it from blowing.
I smell the spring
flowers everywhere.
The breeze will never stop blowing around
the large round
world.

Raina Gagnow :: Grade 5
Lino Lakes Elementary :: Lino Lakes

JOHNNY APPLESEED

Johnny eats the seeds
of plant and life.
Down, down till it
burns hot in his furnace.
New life springs forth
within a life.
Sprouting internally without
control, like a dark
snowball rolling down a hill.
Johnny puts forth new green
life. His leaves protrude and
hide red spheres like a cloud
over the sun.

Brian Petrich :: Grade 8
Oltman Junior High School :: Cottage Grove

It's Everything

It's like an all season
fort. In the summer you
go in shorts. In winter
you go in snowpants,
scarves, jackets, mittens,
boots and caps. It's been
a Star Trek spaceship,
it's been a crocodile's back,
it's been an angry warlock's
plate, it's been a mansion
filled with servants, it's
been everything. With all
the things we need built in—
there's seats, slides, branch
ladders, even a pretend
microphone. You can
eat lunch there. You can eat
a snack there. It's amazing
what a fallen down tree
can be.

Mariah Stember :: Grade 4
Central Elementary :: Bemidji

White Bear Lake

White Bear Lake grins at you because the fish tickle his insides. He laughs at you when you don't catch anything and he eats the worms and leeches off your hook. He hides the fish in the seaweed, so people won't catch them all. He laughs when boats go by because they scratch his back.

The lake is taking off its winter clothing of bluish grey ice and wants to put on his summer coat of blue. The bridges look like ribbons on the coat. The lake tastes and smells fishy. It dreams about the warm summer sun and swimmers. But it gets black and blue from all the people kicking as they swim.

Group Poem :: Grade 3
Bellaire Elementary School :: White Bear Lake

UNTITLED

"You wouldn't want to be the first one to drink from the pump." That is what Mr. Rooney said. He was talking about the pump in the basement of his old school. He said the first person to drink from the pump would get sand in their mouth. I bet he was first as many times as an octopus has legs.

"You know it's true what they say on the Glenwood Inglewood commercials: Glenwood Inglewood since 1884." Even though Mr. Rooney doesn't go back that far, he said that when he was in school they had a Glenwood Inglewood jar in the basement after they had the pump. He said there were paper cups and you would take a paper cup and fill it with water. Mr. Rooney has been living there for about as long as a giraffe's neck, fifty years. He has served on the White Bear Lake School Board for fifteen years. That's a long time!

When Mr. Rooney was little he said it cost ten cents to see a movie! Now it is about $10. He also said you could buy a bike for $8.00 and a car for $1,000.

I would like to be living in White Bear Lake in the 1930s and I wouldn't. I would because I would like to see what it would be like in 1930. I wouldn't because I would rather go to the bathroom inside.

Anna Mason :: Grade 4
Bellaire Elementary :: White Bear Lake

UNTITLED

There was a fire
in the kitchen
says the stove with
soot on it.
The fire spread
rapidly says the
burned door on the
other end of the hallway.
Firemen came say
the warped books
scattered on the
lawn. It wasn't an
electrical fire, say the
lights still hanging
perfectly on the
gray ceiling. It did
not spread fast
say the perfectly
erased boards with
no chalk marks at all.
It did not reach
very high, say
the singed posters
with tops of slightly
melted plastic.
There was a rush
say the skid marks
on the floor. It
was at exactly
10:39 say the
clocks on each wall.

It was cold say
the thick coats
still in the black
lockers.

Kim Stevens :: Grade 8
River Falls Middle School :: River Falls

Duane Moulton — A Rush City Farmer

As I stood outside of Duane Moulton's new house, I looked down the road and saw his old house and barn just down the road. I rang the door bell, and he took my coat and put it in their closet. We sat down at a table and talked. By looking out the window, we could see the land Duane and his family had farmed for years. The high school football and baseball field now stand on land his family used to farm.

He was born on this family farm. His parents were share croppers and were desperately poor. Duane recalled that all of his clothes were homemade. He remembered that he had to go barefoot during the summer; then, when school came, he got one pair of shoes to last him through the year. When he was six, his parents made him go to town and ask the butcher for a soupbone so they could have a meal. A young person had a hard time making money in those days. Duane remembered Gill Nessel's house being built and going there to pick nails out of boards for 5 cents a pound.

There was no TV back in those days and people left the house for entertainment. When Duane was in high school basketball, the auditorium was packed with people wanting to enjoy the thrill of rivalry. He also remembered that on Saturdays farmers would quit work early and then sit on benches in front of the grocery store and tell stories in Swedish while their wives shopped in the stores.

He also described the change in the area since those days. On the dirt road by Kingers, there used to be 18 farms — now there is only one. "The whole Rush city area has only twelve big farms now," he stated sadly. When he was growing up, Rush City had seven churches and seven saloons. Back then people were more church oriented. Back then, before Easter, a high school could even show a movie about Jesus entering Jerusalem. "Now in schools," he stated, "you can't mention anything about religion . . ." The seven churches were always packed on Sundays.

Now, Duane and his son Mark run the family farm together. They are what you call "general farmers." They raise calves up to adults until they are ready for slaughter. The cattle are Angus crossbred with Simmental. The cattle raised on the Moulton farm travel a long distance before they end their journey in a fancy East Coast restaurant. The Moultons also raise up to 1,000 young feeder pigs a year. They also raise alfalfa, corn and oats as animal feed. They try to be self-sufficient.

Duane said that Rush City had its chance to grow. When he was young, Montgomery Wards wanted to put a store in Rush City. Back then a small group of people owned the town, and if they had purchased some larger businesses, Rush City might have grown. Now he feels pessimistic about its future. Many farmers have lost their farms, and he hopes our community can keep its school and hospital.

Times have changed. Now he sees acres of cleared land going back to brush—land that he and his father worked by hand to clear of stumps. This is his home. He farmed it for 51 years. Times have changed.

Ryen Tripp :: Grade 8
Rush City School :: Rush City

WHITE

White is a crayon
coloring a picture of a ghost.

White is chalk
drawing a cloud sitting down
and making fog.

White is snow
floating softly from the sky
getting jumped on by John Jacob Jingle
who makes tracks into the North Pole
and finds a polar bear with white hair
eating a penguin for lunch
and throwing the bones to a walrus
who closes his white teeth around them
goes back to his cave in the ice
trees under water
and flosses his teeth.

Group Poem :: Grade 1
Shirley Hills Elementary :: Mound

I was walking on the soft and sandy beach one day thinking about my oncoming birthday.

The white waves tapped at my feet. I looked up at the pinkish sky, and saw a huge door slung above me.

It was outlined in light green. Its glassy wood complexion fascinated me. A square brass knob stuck out from the side. In its middle was a large knocker shaped like a lion. Its giant jaws looked like it was ready to devour you.

I reached out to touch it, and my hand went right through it! I quickly pulled my hand out, and felt it again. This time, my hand touched a smooth and solid surface.

Judging that I'd never put my hand through it again, I walked around feeling hopeless and that I'd never see what's behind the door.

Then I tripped over something very large. I looked up, feeling a bit dazed, but I got my courage back. I looked up at what I tripped over and caught a glimpse of a golden sparkle.

I pulled on it and it popped out with ease. It was a golden key with a profile of a lion on it.

"Hey," I thought. "This looks like the knocker on the door."

I picked up the key and ran over to the door. I inserted it in the door and held my breath as I slowly turned it in the lock.

I stepped back from the door and paused. "I wonder . . . gosh, if I only knew what was behind that door."

Then I remembered when I opened my mother's cleaning cabinet door. I drank all of her "409" toilet, tub and tile cleaner. Boy, was my mom mad that day!

I giggled, thinking of that silly time. I couldn't go to the children's bazaar because I was spending the weekend in my room.

Many times have I walked through doors I shouldn't have. "But," I thought, "what the heck." And I reached for the brass, square knob.

I turned the knob slowly and heard a soft "click." I cautiously opened the door and looked around.

To my left I saw a beautiful river. An apple tree grew beside it. Orchids surrounded it like a fence letting nothing creep through.

To my right was a courtyard. A statue of a young woman stood in its gardens.

I looked ahead, and that was the most gorgeous sight of all. A golden palace towered before me. Its jeweled draw bridge gleamed. Rubies, emeralds, diamonds and sapphires glittered on its gates. I was in Heaven . . . *I thought.*

I looked towards the door and it vanished. I quickly ran towards the palace.

Then, I stopped. I heard sobbing, it was coming from the river. I softly approached the river. Ducking behind the apple tree I watched intently.

A woman was sitting by the riverside weeping. She looked exactly like the statue in the garden!

The woman was clad in a white robe which reached down to her feet. Her hair was tangled and ratted. And her dark green eyes were filled with tears.

I silently proceeded towards her and lightly tapped her on the shoulder.

"Oh." She sat up with a start. "Who are you?" she asked, "And where did you come from?"

"I'm Erin, I come from the planet Earth. I was walking on the beach and I saw this wierd door. It was locked. So I walked away and tripped over something. It was the key. Now I got through the door and I found you. So that's my story." I stepped back and waited for her reply.

"Oh no," she moaned, "the only way back is jumping over Death Canyon. But no one can do that so my winged unicorn would take you over. But I own it, and I don't own it."

"How could you own something and not own something!" I looked at her, puzzled.

"Simple!" she blurted out. "You see, I haven't told you my story. I am Ganeeva. The planet you are on is Ankora. Two weeks ago this was my kingdom. But now the evil ogre Garnoff owns it. He led a surprise attack on my palace. I was helpless. He quickly gained control of my power and threw me out of my home. So could you help me get my kingdom back. I will help you get home."

"O.k. it's a deal," I said.

"Deal!" she chimed in.

Then she pulled two long swords from her robe, handing one of them to me.

"Keep this with you always," she said. "It will bring you good luck."

So we set off towards the palace . . .

We reached the palace gates and stopped.

"How do we get in?" I asked.

"Follow me," beckoned Ganeeva.

I followed Ganeeva and she led me to a humungus oak tree. She pulled on one of the branches and a hidden door appeared. We quietly walked through it.

A foul smell met my nose as we entered a secret tunnel.

Ganeeva gestured me towards a flight of stairs.

"These lead to the throne room," she said.

I gripped my sword tightly as we slowly climbed the stairs. At the end of the stairs was a trapdoor. Slowly Ganeeva pushed on it and it opened. She quietly pulled herself up through the open space and lifted me up behind her.

"We are behind the throne." Ganeeva said, "When I yell now, we'll run out and stab the ogre through the heart!"

"O.k." I said, "let's get him."

"1-2-3, *now!*" Ganeeva yelled.

We ran out from behind the throne. I took one look at Garnoff and thought "Boy, are you ugly!"

His awful face was covered with warts. His hair was green and dirty. "Yuck!"

Garnoff grabbed his sceptre and pointed it at us.

"Jump!" I yelled, just as a bolt of lightning shot out. And with a flying leap, Ganeeva and I thrust our swords directly through his heart.

With a scream that sounded like an Indian war cry, the ogre dropped dead.

"Hooray!" Ganeeva and I chorused.

Ganeeva led me to a room. There was her beautiful winged unicorn. We coaxed it outside. Ganeeva slipped something around my neck. It was the key.

"Come back and visit me." she said.

"I will!" I said. And I took off on her horse across Death Canyon.

I looked around and I was standing on the beach.

"Good-bye," I said softly.

Erin Anderson :: Grade 5
Long Prairie Schools :: Long Prairie

The raven, king of all, surveys, but then falls sick to a deadly ailment. His friend, mouse, comes to him and asks, "Raven what troubles you so? Why do you cower off of your sky throne?"

"Mouse come to my aid, for I am dying and if a lord of the sky should fall, death and corruption shall come."

"I shall help you lord raven!"

The mouse stretches his arms and fingers and skin fills the empty spaces to form wings. His toe nails become mighty claws and his front teeth elongate to become fangs.

"Hurry mouse, for if panther, king of the night, should come the sky kingdom will be destroyed."

As raven quietly dies the mouse takes the title of Lord of the Sky. He swoops toward the clouds, for he is the *BAT!*

Dale Nelson :: Grade 7
Oltman Junior High School :: St. Paul Park

Not the End, The Beginning

Is the beginning the end
with the pitch black fearless panther,
bolting across the fields,
his eyes shimmering at you in a glare,
the wind makes his graceful figure and black
jacket shine.
He peers in every crack and corner,
and his sleek body slither down for a
cool drink.

There is the hawk who bolts
through the clear blue shining river
of the sky,
the graceful bird screeches down
as the panther, "Where to prey?"
"Down to the river."
The brown hawk does a swooping
dive,
picks up a small mouse in his
sharp beak and flies into the
twilight.

It is not the end.

Stephanie Anderson :: Grade 5
Eisenhower Elementary School :: Hopkins

Atmun Speaks From the Ship

I shiver
from the storm
last night.

Ankle deep
in rainwater
drinking all we can.

I stand
trying to talk
to my people.

Only to be
yelled at and
told to "sit down."

I remember
that night when
my tribe was captured.

Many horrible nights
that water has come
into our hold.

Because the sailor boy didn't
fasten our canvas down.

With the brains of animals
we fight for food
we fight for water.

This horrible boxed–in area
is so cramped and tight
but we will be pulling into harbor soon.

That will be the best day
since my sister's birth.
I cannot wait to smell wonderful fresh air.

Andy Strand :: Grade 5
J.W. Smith Elementary :: Bemidji

THE RABBIT

Nature is blowing,
    a gust of wind.

Rabbit is born

Rabbit makes a quick hop
    through the field of
    grassy sorrow.

He rests in a hollow log
    and finds wolf isn't chasing him.

Rabbit's heart is pounding
    like a lion, roaring in his ear.

Silence now — like a heart breaking.

Rabbit's fur coat is as soft as
    silky rainbow colors.

Eyes glowing like flickering candles.

Hops as high as the sky,
    he jumps into the heart of night.

All I can see is a cloud-like
    fluffy tail.

Anna Mountain :: Grade 4
Royal Oaks Elementary School :: Woodbury

THE RABBIT

Silver glitter, stay in
the sky. The shy rabbit
is cold. His soft, dirty grey
fur is growing slowly.
    Silver glitter stay.

Light breeze, please don't scatter
the colored leaves so
the lettuce will be
buried. He must be hungry.
    Light breeze, please.

Fall, stay light a few more hours.
The rabbit that
jerked at every sound
is lost and may
some day be found.
    Fall, stay light.

Lara Gerhardson :: Grade 5
J. W. Smith Elementary School :: Bemidji

THE FAWN

I could hear my brothers laughing.
I was way out in front of them,
walking briskly, pulling out weeds
fast so I could get to the water first.
I saw something stir
in the wheat field to my right.
Suddenly, the wheat jumped up,
a blur of gold, then it disappeared.
A fawn, no taller than the wheat itself,
bounded away from danger.
I could hear him calling for his mother.
I was crying silently for him to come back.
He heard me. He stopped and studied me with curiosity.
Slowly, he swam toward the bean field,
only his head sticking out
of the ocean of wheat.
He continued marching toward me,
now his entire body and lanky legs were visible.
I couldn't breathe. I cautiously knelt down,
making myself the same size as him.
Closer, closer, I could count the spots.
Closer, closer, I could see the fear, curiosity and innocence
in his huge brown eyes. His ears and tail
too large for his body.
Closer, closer, his wet muzzle met
my sweaty, salty palm.
I snapped back to reality.
"Get out of here," I shouted,
jumping up and throwing
my arms at him.
His frail body sprinted
back to the golden waters,
his white tail waving
like a flag of surrender.

"And don't ever do that again," I whispered.
"You'll get yourself into trouble."
A single tear rolled down my cheek
as my beautiful little fawn
bounded out of sight.

Corrine Sloot :: Grade 10
GFW High School :: Winthrop

UNTITLED

In my deerstand
I wait
I wait
I wait in the trees
The deer comes.
Big
Rack
Points
Kill me.
I aim the gun
At the heart
I squeeze the
Big
Rack
Points
I squeeze the
Points
I squeeze the
Big Rack Points
I slowly squeeze
The fields are covered with snow.
I am starving.
I squeeze the
Kill me.
Big Points
I am starving
in the heart
covered with snow I
Squeeze
the trigger
I feel the kick
in the heart

Dean Engen :: Grade 8
Marshall County Central :: Newfolden

WETLAND

As I strut through
the lush green marsh grass
As I run through
the shallow streams
As I wallow
in the fallen leaves
I stop
and think
I get up again
and run freely
until I stumble to the ground
I stop
and gaze
at the cottony clouds
and wonder if
    I should ever
go home.

Bill Wood :: Grade 5
Gatewood Elementary School :: Minnetonka

THE CLIMB

He looked up with perseverance at the seemingly insurmountable obstacle before him. He had been readying himself for years just to look up like this at the rocky face of Devil's Tower. And hopefully looking down in a few long hours.

The man was tall and muscular, with short, slick dark hair. He wore nothing but a blue jumpsuit and climber's boots, and carried only a water flask and a sandwich. He would have been considered a daredevil by any normal person, but this— freeclimbing—was his hobby.

It was hot, the hottest it had been all summer, and even though it was still early morning, the sun was already beating down on the man and was making beads of sweat appear on his forehead.

He had studied this massive rock structure thoroughly, looking for the best possible place to ascend. This was doubly important for him—he didn't have ropes to save him if he fell. Of course, the man had conquered these fears years ago, and now thought of safety ropes as extra weight, more bulk.

A crow screeching out its mating call jarred him out of his reverie, and he turned his attention again to the rocky structure, going straight up toward the puffy white clouds above. He took a deep breath, and stepped up on the first of the few boulders he would have to cross before he actually started to climb.

It took him about fifteen minutes—he was conserving energy for the real climb. One last time he looked up, then started climbing spider-like up the tower.

The climb was hard from the very beginning. The climber used the jamming technique of jamming his boots in the various cracks, always staying vertical and keeping his body off the rock whenever possible. Without ropes, if he got stretched out on the cliff face and could not see the hand or footholds, he would be doomed.

A whiff of rotting flesh made him dangerously nauseous, and when he looked down he saw vultures at a moose carcass. He was about twenty meters off the ground—only 244 meters to go. The climber was already above tree level, looking over the pines and thorn trees at the beautiful, if desolate, scenery beyond. Occasional hikers happened to glance up and gasp, while little children pointed, and rushed to try to climb the boulders around the tower and be like the 'the climbing person.'

The climber had now found a chimney, a shaft enclosed on two or three sides, going up about fifteen meters. He wedged himself in, using pressure he created against both sides to raise him, meter by meter, up the shaft.

A few meters from the top of the chimney was a small ledge. When he raised his head above it, he instantly flinched back— almost falling—while a long coiled form lashed out at him. He slipped, and panic flooded his mind, but his trained reasoning took over and he summed up the situation. The only way around the snake was down again, and that would take up much valuable time and energy. The rattling of the snake almost induced panic again. He could see the shadow swaying back and forth, waiting.

Then he had an idea. He tore off his belt, and started flailing at the snake with it. It flipped over—a little too far. The snake toppled off the ledge and plummeted down the shaft. He instantly heard the screech of vultures as they closed in.

A little more cautiously, he climbed onto the ledge. The man grasped his water flask and drank deeply. Sweat was pouring down his face, making little pools in the rock. And making the place stink as well.

After a few minutes, he got up again and climbed the rest of the way up the shaft. A blast of hot air almost sent him smashing down on the rocks below. The cliff face was smooth here, but there was a small crack traversing it. He grasped it firmly, and exerted pressure with his legs much like he did in the chimney. The man had learned this five years ago in college at a sports club in Arizona.

That had been where he had met Cynthia. The thought of her, alone at home, made him wonder why he was doing this. But this had always been his goal—first to freeclimb Devil's

Tower. Placing these thoughts out of his mind, he went back to work.

He was about one-third of the way up the tower, having about 164 meters to go. He proceeded up the crack, sometimes having to execute tricky maneuvers to stay on the rock.

About half of the way up, he came upon a narrow ledge leading to a small opening in the rock. Upon further investigation, he found that it extended two meters inward. This kind of thing on Devil's Tower was practically unknown! The exhausted climber pulled himself in. It smelled musty inside, but was shady and cool. The sun had already reached its zenith and was heading down again toward the horizon.

All passersby of the monument looked like ants now, but the man could still hear the honking horns and squealing tires of cars in the parking lot below. A vulture startled him with a scream. He took out his food and slowly ate it, his body sucking up the nourishing energy it provided.

Ten minutes later, he was up and climbing again, using the jamming technique again to proceed up to 180 of the 264 total meters of the tower. He was already anticipating success, which was dangerous, but he could hardly help it.

Circling crows and vultures mingled overhead in a strange dance. Their screeching penetrated his concentration, which was rare, and he paused for a moment to catch his breath and regain his thoughts.

It was getting darker as the climber passed the 220 meter mark. The clouds passed thicker around the drooping sun. He was really getting tired now, and his eyes, bloodshot from the howling updraft, strained for the sight of the last rock, the final exertion.

He was thinking more and more of Cynthia as he proceeded climbing up the tower. He had to make it—if he didn't, Cynthia would have to live alone, without him. The man couldn't bear the thought of it. All the more determined, he picked up his pace as if superhuman and burst up to 235 meters.

All sound and movement below was completely gone. The

only break in the silence was the howling wind and screeching birds. Twenty-four meters to go.

Now he could see the top! He could see the summit! The end was in sight. Ten meters to go.

He found a hold with his hand, then with his foot. Look — hand, foot. Look — hand, foot. His fingers searched for cracks, feet for footholds. Five meters to go.

He strained, every muscle stretching to the maximum of ability. His arm inched up, fingers closed — and he did it! He grasped the top of Devil's Tower! He pulled himself up slowly, getting lost in the exhilaration of the moment. He raised his arm in a victory whoop. A scrabble of rock fell. He widened his eyes in shock — and slipped.

Everything stopped. Everything got silent instantly. The birds stopped screeching and hovered in the air or landed on the tower. Even the wind tapered off to a light breeze.

After a few seconds, things started again. Time was resumed, and peace returned to Devil's Tower.

Tim Bretl :: Grade 7
Blake Middle School :: Hopkins

UNTITLED

I am like a cat, green eyes
searching for something to play with,
someone to prey on.
Come closer and let me bare my claws
and rip you to pieces.
Come closer and let me tear your skin
from your body with my teeth.
Let me taste your flesh and blood,
and know I thrive on it.
I thrive on it, and you are not the first
and may not be the last.

I am an egg, fragile, so easily broken,
but left to rot when the deed is done.
I feel myself in the hands of a person,
treated so carefully.
Of course this person is using me.
I bring a price.
I feel the entrapment of the walls
I am placed carefully inside of.
I want to rebel, but can't.
Soon I am in the hands
of another careless person
and then it's all over
as I hit the burning pavement
of modern America, and am slowly tramped
and fried until I am nothing
but a lost memory full of dreams.

I am a boomerang.
Throw me as far and fast
as you like, cast me away from you
and see that I always come back
haunting you.
You will never have to come after me.

Just as you think you may have to,
I will be there.
Just as you think you have
gotten rid of me, I will be there.
Just as I thought I could escape,
I will be there.

Brandy Elf :: Grade 12
McGregor High School :: McGregor

I am scared of
gushing water
and the booming
thunder combined
with lightning.
But now it is gone.
I'm glad it is gone
especially
the sea serpent.

Charlie Sequin :: Grade 2
Lakeview Elementary :: Robbinsdale

"How did it go today?"

" 'Twas the same. 'Tis odd not a soul 'er heard of the Enchanted Sword of Ire." The old woman who sat across the worn, but lovingly taken care of, table just shook her head. The movement caused a few more strands of hair to fly out in various directions adding to her already disheveled appearance.

"I think you need some help. Now, please, don't go getting on your high and mighty preaching stand. Don't tell me that all you need is that crossbow and that bag of feathers you call a bird."

"You be bein' right as exactly as always. I think it be time to find him, Gramma." The girl stood, shook out the midnight cloak that so cleverly hid her gender. Just before she turned to leave her gramma, years wiser than she, spoke.

"Remember to sing as you go. Remember to live up to your name, Larksong." Larksong nodded, looked lovingly at the room, so much her gramma, perhaps for the last time. She took time to absorb all the details. The cheery fire, the spotless floor and shelves. Sighing she walked to her gramma, gave her a long hug, then called to the preening, brightly colored lark.

"Latisha." The bird, in apparent annoyance, barely glanced at her with her bright blue eyes. Then she alighted on her mistress' slender shoulder. Larksong walked slowly to the door with calm steps. Turning she gazed at the room and the woman; one that she had been raised in and one that had raised her. Without a sound, she turned and fled into the night.

"I understand, my child. It is your destiny." But she still shook her head and shed the tear shimmering below the surface.

* * * * *

Kel looked up. Someone was coming. Then a beautiful voice floated along the light breeze. Then the voice, so pure but melancholy, started singing a song. It weaved a web, fine and sheenlike, around his soul. The sound drew him out of the fragile green forest. A figure draped in a midnight cloak was walking towards him. The multicolored lark on her, deduced for the haunting voice was feminine, was copying the song but the sound was nothing like that of the woman's. She happened to look up at the very moment he started strolling, at a gentle gait, towards her. Fear showed in her eyes for the brief second he saw them, then she was off running like the deer he hunted. Matter of fact she was running faster than any deer. She was thinking no doubt that she was in trouble. Slowing he drew out an arrow, deftly fitting it on the string of his worn longbow, paused then let it fly. It sliced through the cloak flapping behind her, finally coming to rest in a sturdy sapling. Then, horrified, watched her snap back, strike the tree, and crumple to the stony ground. Carefully, he picked her delicate body, shocked at the strength he felt. He noticed she was breathing and he took a calming one. He smelled the sweet scent of raspberries, mingling in the air.

In a faraway castle, a tiny man hopped about, screaming and cursing the fates. Now the two halves of the whole that would destroy him if given the chance, were together. But if one were to die . . . smiling an evil grin he pointed an incredibly long finger at Kel. The one word he whispered only made the grin eviler.

"Death."

Kel was still undecided what to do with the girl, when he heard a strange out of place noise in the usually quiet forest. Turning, he saw a ball of black light coming straight towards him. It bounced off the girl's cloak and flew harmlessly away. But the girl woke up and promptly screamed. He dropped her and she landed in a graceless heap at his feet. She cursed, picked herself up and dusted off her cloak. Then she looked up and smiled.

"You aren't going to hurt me, are you?" At his nod, she smiled again, "In that case my name be bein' Larksong and this be Latisha." She touched her shoulder, then without preamble sang a high clear note. The lark he had glimpsed before dived out of nowhere to land on her shoulder.

"What be bein' your name?" He found her curiosity interesting.

"Kel. Kel Kertilon." The brightness in her eyes faded, her voice had changed subtly.

"Give me your hand." For a reason he felt drawn to do it, so he did. He instantly learned of her struggle. She had to find the sword which was being held by a sorcerer. The moment passed and the brightness in her eyes came back and the brightness in the large ruby around her neck died. He had just noticed the ruby and its intricate setting. Larksong smiled.

"Are you with me?"

"Forever and a day." He barely heard her mutter under her breath, "It could come to that."

* * * * *

They had been walking, no, trudging for the past two days. Not that they had ever gone hungry or never had a village where they couldn't stay anywhere. Her voice had been making sure of that. But now they hadn't seen a village or for that matter anyone. Right about now it was getting a wee bit monotonous, and the scenery wasn't to blame. Kel hadn't said so much as a whisper, he was becoming a bit monot . . .

"There it is." Larksong's eyes looked up and to the right, but her body didn't move. Unbelievably the castle was only a quarter of a mile away, and they managed to get there in a few minutes. But to their mutual shock and horror there was obviously no way they could get in.

"Oh, faith and . . . well, now, what do we do?"

"If you feel up to it we could go through that window way up there." Twenty minutes later they were in a large main hall with massive wood doors. Larksong gave no announcement, just burst into the room behind those doors. The tiny man stopped hopping around and simply stared dumbfounded. She smiled, then as Kel witnessed before the brightness just faded away. The ruby around her neck started glowing then a form appeared, red as the ruby itself. The voice that had spoken to him back in the forest, spoke to him again. It commanded, 'Give her your hand, she needs your strength.' Kel gave Larksong his hand and saw the little wizard's face turn pale. The form finally became solid, it was that of a young woman. She was dressed all in ruby red and looked exactly like Larksong. She had the same blue-black hair as Larksong and the same blue beyond blue eyes. She walked towards the mage and spoke.

"You loved me once. That love will destroy you."

"No, no, no. I just came to full power." The little wizard screamed. Undaunted, the woman pointed to the ruby necklace and the little mage disappeared. The woman walked over to them, pulled Larksong aside, and whispered softly in her ear. Larksong carefully pulled the necklace off and turned to him and smiled. Then she walked out the door. When he finally caught up to her, he burst out.

"What did she say?"

"Oh, she be sayin' something along the lines that me Gramma might awantin' to be meetin' you." They both smiled.

"And what might you be thinkin'?" Larksong laughed.

"I thinks me Gramma just might be wantin' that, too." So, arm in arm they strolled out of the castle and back towards home.

Robyn Johnson-Welch :: Grade 8
Moorhead Junior High School :: Moorhead

Untitled

The sweet melody of a piano
sings me to sleep
the keys open up a new world
A world of happiness and joy
In this world, there is no
discrimination
of black and white
just harmony
a blending of colors that
sound so nice

Stephanie Casperson :: Grade 9
Salk Junior High School :: Elk River

The Cleaner

When cleaning your house
you must clean your room,
your kitchen, bathroom,
clean your basement, your
sister's room. When cleaning
the sky so high you need a
ladder to polish the stars.
You've got to make them shine.
You must give the sun a new
flame and tell the sun to
give the moon more light.
You must shake the clouds
clean and that is how to
clean your house or the
universe. That is the way
you do it. So take my advice and
do what I say—to clean
anywhere—just do it.

Ian Graf :: Grade 2
Hale School :: Minneapolis

Shawn got his driver's license.
The U.S. invaded Panama.
Called Strut the ultimate damaging name.
Hurricane Hugo wiped out Charleston.
Daren and Jason took second place in the Dairy Days
        softball tournament.
Brandon and Shawn did a Chinese fire drill.
Tyson got beat by Buster Douglas.
Strut gave Shawn a bloody nose.
Shawn was Prince Jonathan.
EVERYONE went to the RTR State Tournament.
Bush went to Colombia and came back alive.
Rushdie came out of hiding.
Ayatollah Khomeini died and was pulled out of his coffin
        onto the street.
Jacob Wetterling was kidnapped.
The Berlin Wall came down.
Chinese students were killed in the square.
Daren got second in the district track meet.
Bullets got eight root canals.
I saw the 49ers win the Super Bowl.

Group Poem :: Grade 9
RTR High School :: Tyler

UNTITLED

The flag with its red
blood and white bandages
and the great stars
guiding the way for
the soldiers on their
way home. The blue is
the sky that watches over
them.

Robert Hostrawser :: Grade 6
Caledonia Elementary School :: Caledonia

LIFE STORY

I decided to be born, in the hot climate
of July. I decided I will be a girl instead
of a boy. I decided to go to school when I
was five instead of six.

I turned into a lady of seventeen.

I strolled down the halls like a beauty queen.

I remember the day so long ago, a fog
in my head, then it was washed away.

I decided to leave my family of five, to
see the ocean, to smell the breeze, to change
my life, to take away the past.

I decided to live, like a wild man, I decided
to be free and not hold my parents' hands.

I decided to leave, decided on a plan. I
will take a plane to a world beyond seas,
and you just wait and see my friend, I've
decided to be me.

Terrie Sanz :: Grade 10
Alternative Learning Center :: St. Paul Park

Matt strode down the barren road in Sticksville, Rochester. He was thinking heavily about Nintendo. Matt thought of Nintendo as his Bluebird of Happiness; leaving it was his Chicken of Depression. His uncombed brown hair and glasses attracted nobody he liked. He longed to have video game characters leap from the screen and befriend him. His best friends were power-ups on Super Mario Bros. 3. People stayed away from him like a snake from a mongoose. His bad temper made him even less popular. At Outskirts Elementary, he held the record for discipline slips, most of them for fights. Few kids insulted him and got away with it. It was his addiction to fights that had gotten him into this mess. He was headed for a conference at his home. He approached his house. Peeking in the front window, he saw the adults clustered around the dining room table. This was his last chance. He took it.

Quick as a flash, he threw open the outside door to the cellar. He descended, clearing a path. He knew he'd need this soon. He slipped open the door at the other end, closed it, and made a break for the door to his room and sanctuary. He made it, threw himself in, locked the door, and turned on the NES.

In the kitchen, Matt's parents were waiting for him. Then they heard music from Super Mario 3 float down the hall. Matt was in for it.

Matt, however, wasn't playing Nintendo. He was packing. He was going to hike from Rochester, MN, to Detroit, MI. That was the closest place Matt knew of where his dream could really come true. Matt wanted to boast his Nintendo skills to a large city. In Detroit, the Nintendo World Championships were going to be held. Matt's few friends had agreed to help him. Matt stashed the luggage in the closet, then headed out to the conference.

Matt entered the room. He saw a note on his favorite chair. It read: "Matthew: You will be sent to a military academy. Your parents." Matt was desperate. He ran for the telephone and dialed Jesse's phone number.

"Jesse!" Matt screamed!

"What?"

"My parents are sending me to a military school! We gotta make the break tonight!"

"Okay, I'll call the others, you get the food."

Matt agreed. He snuck to the fridge. In five minutes, a jar of pickles, two loaves of bread, a plate of leftover turkey, two bottles of Mountain Dew and a few boxes of cookies were in the cooler and downstairs.

At eleven o'clock, the five escapees gathered in Matt's cellar. There they were, each with a different talent that would serve them well: Matt was there, of course, with a cool head in most cases. Jesse was ascending the stairs to the outer cellar door and coming back down. He had knowledge about science and also had ESP and mind-over-matter. Phillip had a checklist and amazing physical abilities. Noah was outside loading the gear into his brother's car. He had an outstanding knowledge of the wooded areas of the states. Noah's brother Steve was the only one old enough to drive. The five of them were making final preparations for the trip. When they had everything, they split.

Steve's black ATV drove deep into the woods. When the boys found a suitable campsite, they set to work. Jesse's mind power gathered perfect firewood. Matt pitched the tents and unpacked the bags. Noah built a fire; three, really: an overnight fire, a field fire and a crisscross fire. Phil explored the woods very quickly and set up some traps. Steve parked his truck near the tents, then lifted the tents right up onto the back of his truck so as for easy departure. Then the five of them sat down for some food.

Matt's parents had not wasted a moment. As soon as they found him missing, they contacted the parents of the other four. Then the eight adults alerted the police and searched their homes for clues. Then, two days after the boys had left, their parents set out on their trail. Matt figured this. So he decided to split the woods with his companions. Once they reached a town, they would repaint Steve's truck, check into a motel, and set off again.

In the motel, Matt explained the rest of his plan. They were in Wisconsin, and they were very close. So they would check into motels every night, sign in under a false name, and maybe get some help. At the motels, he would practice the games needed in NWC. "If we can win the NWC, we can get home via train," he explained. Just then, came a knock on the door! Matt cautiously opened the door a crack and peeked out. Five girls stood outside the door.

"Excuse us, but we couldn't help overhearing," said one.

"That's okay, just don't tell anybody," was Matt's reply.

"You can come in, if you want," added Steve. After a long discussion, the ten got acquainted with each other. When Matt found out that Cindi, the first girl, was also going to register in the NWC, he invited her to try her luck. In five minutes she had collected 50 coins on Super Mario Bros., scored a lap on Rad Racer, and gotten to level 9 on Tetris. Matt did it just as good, but in four minutes. The heat was on. Two days to the NWC!

"Well, Matt, here's the convention center. Are you sure you want to go through with this?" asked Noah.

Matt nodded. He wanted to save his voice for the crowd. After the two contestants registered, Matt headed for the Power Walk. He tried his hand at Final Fantasy, Super C and Rescue Rangers. Then it was competition time. One after another, the contestants played to the max of their abilities, kicking Koopas, weaving through traffic, twisting 4-bars. In the end, Matt came out on top. When asked about his secret, Matt grinned, and replied, "Well, I guess I have the NES advantage without the NES Advantage."

Mike Speck :: Grade 5
Winona Central Elementary :: Winona

1: THE CARS ZOOMED ALL AROUND THE TOWN 2:

4:		
WHOLE		SPITTING
PLACE		EXHAUST
SHOOK		IN
RAPIDLY	T O X I C	THE
WITH		PATH
A	W A S T E	OF
BOOM		OTHER
AND		CARS.
A		BIG
BANG		TANKS
THEY		WERE
CRASHED		DROPPED
CRASHED	T O X I C C O.	DOWN
TO		DOWN
THE		DOWN
BOTTOM		INTO
THERE		THE
THEY		DEPTHS
STAYED	MADE IN THE U.S.A.	OF
FOR		THE
YEARS.		OCEAN.

3: DOWN TO THE VERY BOTTOM OF THE OCEAN. "CRASH!"

Gwendolyn Burghardt :: Grade 5
Washington Elementary :: New Ulm

Introduction:	We went into an alley, and this is what we saw:
JON:	(Whistling) Here we are. The alley of terror.
REBECCA:	Do we have to do this? This looks unsafe!
DENA:	Come on, frady cat!
EVERYBODY:	Chicken!
AMANDA:	Rebecca's right! There's street people everywhere!
MOLLY:	What are we going to do?
JON:	You guys are going to interview a street person, I made sure there's one for each of you!
SARAH:	Jon, can I go first? I have my eye on that cute boy!
JON:	Okay, then Dena, you're next.
SARAH:	Can I go?
JON:	No, not yet.
DENA:	I pick Jessica.
JESSICA:	Why me?
NARRATOR:	Once everyone was picked, Jon excused them to go.
JESSICA:	HI! We are interviewing you guys. Can I ask you some questions?
BOY:	Sure.
JESSICA:	My name is Jessica.
BOY:	Well, nice to meet ya! Mine is Jon.
JESSICA:	Really? My director's name is Jon.
JON:	COOL!
JESSICA:	So how old are you?
JON:	15. How old are you?
JESSICA:	I'm 15 too.
JON:	So are you going to ask me some questions or what?
JESSICA:	Oh, yeah! I forgot!
JON:	Snap out of it.

(JESSICA and JON laugh. Everyone looks over at them.)

JESSICA and JON:	SORRY.
JESSICA:	Why are you on the street at age 15?
JON:	Well, I got beat on, so I just moved out.
JESSICA:	Oh. How long have you been on the street?
JON:	7 months.
JESSICA:	Are you scared?
JON:	YEAH! I mean you never know when you're going to die. I'm scared every minute of my life.
JESSICA:	How do you get food?
JON:	Well, there's always the dumpster.
JESSICA:	Want to take a walk? I will still ask you questions.
JON:	OK, let's walk!
JESSICA:	You want to meet Jon? I mean my director.
JON:	Sure! I'd love to.
JESSICA:	Jon?
JON (Director):	Hi! Is this the boy you're interviewing?
JESSICA:	Yes. Jon, this is Jon.
JON:	Hi.
JESSICA:	Can we take a walk?
JON (Director):	Sure, but watch out! There are muggers out there!
JON:	I'll keep her safe.
	(JESSICA and JON look at each other)
JON (Director):	O.K.
JESSICA and JON:	Thanks, Jon!
JON:	Come on!
JESSICA:	Sorry. Hey! Wait up!
	(She starts running faster.)
JON:	Sorry.
JESSICA:	That's okay.
JON:	Let's go in here.
JESSICA:	O.K.
	(JON makes a quick move and grabs JESSICA)

JON: Come here, Jessica. You're going to like this.
                Come here!
JESSICA: Jon what are you doing? NO! YOU BIG STU-
                PID LITTLE BRAT!!
JON: You're going to pay for that!
JESSICA: JON! HELP!
JON: SHUT UP!
                (JON (Director) comes running)
JON (Director):JESSICA!
JON: Get away old Man!
JON (Director):Leave her alone! Let her go!
JON: Make me!
                (JON (Director) kicks JON and frees JESSICA.
                JESSICA starts biting.)
JON: OUCH!! You little brat! I'm bleeding!
                (JESSICA slips out of his grip.)
JESSICA: YOU STUPID LITTLE . . .
JON (Director):Go get the police!
                (JON (Director) punches JON. He falls to the ground.
                JESSICA goes to a pay phone, calls police. The police
                    come over, and she tells them the story.)
NARRATOR: Jon was arrested and Jessica and Jon were in the
                paper and they never went to that alley again.

Jessica Buchta :: Grade 4
Beaver Lake Elementary School :: North St. Paul

Untitled

You look out a window
it's like being a prisoner
in a castle. I smell
the nice smells of the melting snow.
The people are like brooms
sweeping the streets,
the skyscrapers
are like big spears
killing nobody—just stuck
in the ground.
The city, in a way,
can be smaller
than you.

Kipp Vanness :: Grade 4
Webster Magnet School :: St. Paul

A Moment in Time

As I am walking down 2nd Street, I can smell the fresh new tar from the street. The sky is as blue as a jaybird, and the clouds like cream.

I then can see Pipen's house, the white house with black steps. To the left is their garage. It has a few bikes and a red lawn mower. I then pass the Homes' house with a big beautiful brown garage and a large blue door in the front with silver bells hanging from the white screen door.

I notice a branch. It is about the length of a baseball bat, but skinny as a baby's wrist. I want to be a baseball player. I think I'd like to play for the Minnesota Twins, smelling the aroma of butter on popcorn, hearing the roar of the crowd, and seeing the ball fly out of the ball park. Yeah, that's what I want to be, a ball player.

The next house is the Brower's house. A two storey high blue house with a mini-garden at the side. In the mini-garden grow strawberries and big daisies, lots of them.

My home, I guess that's what you'd call it, is a tin shack. It gets very cold at night, no electricity, no running water, and most of all no heat! My family is homeless. This is all we got right now. We'll be moving in a month. I suppose we will go to a big city, where there's drugs and violence.

I'm 15 and my brother is 16 years old. We help farmers with their work to support our family. Some nights we eat and some nights we don't. My dad usually goes fishing at the Minnesota River but sometimes he doesn't catch anything.

My parents aren't working now, but they're looking for jobs. Both my parents didn't go to college, and my dad dropped out of high school when he was 17.

It is almost sunset. The sky grows darker, and the clouds vanish. You can see the stars twinkle and sparkle in the sky. The big red sun fades, like dying, behind the hills. The sun looks like it is hiding from something. I wish I could hide from everything.

Paul Mauer :: Grade 8
GFW Middle School :: Fairfax

NUMBERS

The big numbers stunk like socks as the garbage
can tipped over. The sour milk turned into
letters. The fogged up glasses clouded up
the sky. Words were multiplying by twos &
threes as my hair was subtracting from my
head. Numbers add up to the shoes that
are hooked to chairs. We divide the numbers
amongst ourselves while the Beaver floats around.
Ice cream melts on the chair & adds a different
look. The numbers multiply themselves
by halves as Ms. Shiely turns thirty.

Jody Kolbeck :: *Grade 7*
Oltman Junior High School :: *St. Paul Park*

A girl dashed through the thick fog on a hillside in Vermont, bending and ducking to get through the forest. Something shone through her tightly clenched fingers, barely shining in the sunlight.

She showed her mom the golden cylinder she had found while hiking by the creek. Her mom, wide-eyed with excitement, held it in her hands with passion, but decided that they must turn it over to the museum.

They drove to the local museum, speeding down the twisted road as they grew closer to Burlington. When they pulled up to the museum the girl tucked it away in a pocket, went inside and handed it over to some archeologists.

The archeologists were intrigued as they pried off the lid, then peered in when it popped off. They found a scroll written on old, brittle paper in an unreadable language. They called in an outside archeologist from New York, Tennessee Hawkins, who was experienced in this field.

Tennessee's tall figure drew a dark shadow over the scroll for hours, examining every corner and character. 11:37 p.m., he wrapped up the scroll and put it in its golden case. Then he went and told the other archeologists he would examine the land tomorrow. He walked to his car and drove away.

As he drove down the twisted road he thought of the possibilities that lay behind that piece of history and what it could prove.

CHAPTER 2

The next morning he drove to a spot in the road where he could park his car. He got out a bag that was full of equipment; out of it he took a map of the area, compass, machete, and a gun which was a habit to carry after being shot at in the Amazon. Quickly he loaded his pockets and set off up the hill.

The miles and miles of forest were very thick; his knife lashed back and forth to get through the weeds. On his way to the stream he encountered many animals which he let walk by while he stood motionless watching. When he got to the stream around high noon the temperature had increased about 15 degrees, and the fog had lifted. He looked around for about two hours, then took a break.

When he rested, he noticed the noise he thought was his own, wasn't. He ignored it, but it came calling back in his ear. Something was stalking him like a wolf in the moonlight.

"Who's there?"

No answer, and all he saw was a rigid dark figure standing on the other side of the stream. Then he saw it gleam; the sun shone through the trees as he looked down the point of a gun.

"There will be no competitors," the figure said in a low ambitious voice. Tennessee's hand longed for his gun and crept to it slowly, but before he could reach it he was stunned by a bullet piercing through his shoulder and blowing it from its socket. The bullet came from the stranger's gun. As Tennessee leaned forward in pain, he hit his head on a rock and rolled into the stream unconscious.

He woke up choking. Drenched, he dragged himself out of the water. There was no sign of civilization.

He was in a valley, surrounded by forests. The river came to a bend where it had dropped him off and then disappeared into the forest. He wrung his clothes and tried to make a fire, but his matches were soaked. The sun was setting, and the temperature dropped. He made a small shelter, curled up, and went to sleep.

When he woke up, his clothes were dry, and he noticed his shoulder, numb. It was thoroughly cleansed from the river. He wrapped it up in a ripped sleeve from his shirt. It was a deep wound, and it would take several weeks to heal. Still, he wondered why anybody would shoot him. He was just looking for artifacts. Or was it something more?

His map was ruined, machete and compass lost, and he was on unfamiliar ground.

He got his things together and started up the hill. It was a long climb, but it was essential to get out of the valley. On his way up he noticed many rocks. There was one long flat rock he walked across that gave a hollow effect. At first he thought he was insane, but then he tapped on it again, and he still heard it. He gave it a push, and it started to move. How could he move such a large rock? He pushed more, and then he saw something unbelievable—a fraction of an entrance to a cave. He heard a crack behind him. Turned around and saw him.

"Sit down, Mr. Hawkins. I wish to speak to you."

Tennessee snatched his gun and pointed it at the man. "I don't know who you are or what you want, but just keep to your business!"

"You don't need your gun, so put it away and we'll talk."

"Why did you shoot me?"

"It was an accident. The trigger slipped!?"

"No, you did it for a reason, and I want to know why!"

". . . you . . . are looking for artifacts which I long for."

"I don't know—"

"Shut up! I have a map that shows everything but where it is . . ."

"Listen, I really . . . what's your name anyway?

"It's MacAvoy. Now tell me, where is it?"

"I don't know."

"You lie!"

Tennessee took off up the hill with bullets shooting behind him.

"I will kill you, Hawkins!"

As Tennessee dashed over the top of the hill and down it, he came to a screeching halt only to be surrounded by a tribe of what looked like Native Americans. Then he heard the footsteps behind him.

"You found them . . . All my life, and you found them!" screamed MacAvoy.

The natives took them both prisoners and led them down long winding caves into the hillside.

"Do you know who they are, Hawkins?"

"If I knew, I wouldn't be here!"

"They're Dacanyos, a lost civilization in the hillside of Vermont, never recorded, never put into history, just lost!"

"And we're dead if we don't get out of here!"

CHAPTER 3

The Dacanyos led them to a huge room where all the caves went. It was lined with raw gold. In front of them, high up on what looked like an alter, sat a civilized person who looked as if he was from the 1920's but hadn't aged.

"Hello gentlemen, we have been expecting you." He said it in a low calming voice.

Tennessee walked up to him. "Hey, Yo! Listen, if you could get me out of here, because you see—"

"I will do no such thing!" He stood up and shoved Tennessee off the ten foot altar onto the rocky floor back first. Tennessee stood up gasping in pain, grabbed his gun, aimed for the man's throat and shot the bullet in dead aim . . . It did nothing. The man laughed and Tennessee stumbled closer; where the bullet had gone through the flesh not even a cut remained.

"Ha! You fool you can do nothing to kill me, for I . . . I and my people are time travelers! I am in the past, and you, you are in the future; yet we meet by intersecting on the lines of time!"

"I . . . don't . . . believe you, you're insane!"

"Believe it, for you have nothing else to go by. We can kill you at anytime, but you can't interfere with us. It can be reversed also if you come to my time—"

"Which is?"

". . . The past. But now, you must die, for you have interfered with our time circle. Take them away!"

MacAvoy and Tennessee struggled but could not overcome the power of the tribe. They were dragged back through the caves into a small room with only one entrance. They were locked up, with wood bars across the front. MacAvoy was in awe, and Tennessee was tired. Then the man walked up, on the other side of the bars.

"You see, I'm in the same position as you gentlemen . . . have you ever heard of the Bermuda Triangle, or the Great Pyramid? Well . . . there are only three places in the world where time travel is possible, and you're in one of them. These are mysteries to the world. 'Another plane lost,' or 'Another person missing.' But you see they aren't lost; they've been lost in time . . . warped. 'The hills of Vermont'—that's what they told me. Now I, as you, are lost in time. Every 24 hours our time, the world as we know it advances 67 . . . years. I come from the year 1923 which means you come from the year 1990. I've only been here one day, 67 years, but I don't age. Neither will you."

Tennessee crawled up in a sitting position. "How did you know? . . . 67 years?"

He chuckled. "I have the same scroll you do." He held it up. "Just because I have it doesn't mean it disappears from history. This is the key, what draws people to this place. Unless it is destroyed it will always appear 67 years in the future."

"But how did you know?"

"I had the natives decipher it. They speak every language in the world. We are now in the year? . . . 2004. You will have to be killed tomorrow. I will mine the gold myself!"

"You're crazy . . ."

"I must go."

The man walked away. Tennessee and MacAvoy fell asleep.

CHAPTER 4

They woke up. The man was sitting outside the prison.

"Hello gentlemen, do you know why you woke up at the same time? We are in the year 2057; we will soon have a visitor."

MacAvoy yawned. "Why don't we know your name?"

"It is impossible, try saying yours."

"Interesting?"

Meanwhile, Tennessee thought of a way to escape. He thought of only one way.

"Ahh! Gentlemen, the warp is now opening. It will be open only for two minutes."

At that moment Tennessee drew his gun and shot the bullets right through four branches that held them in the room. He ran and crashed through them. MacAvoy, not far behind. He ran into the tunnel that led them there with only one thought, free.

"After them!" The man yelled to the natives. They followed with bows strung.

Tennessee looked for light ahead. Several times he shot back at them. Time was running out; 57 seconds remained before the door shut. He changed courses many times, tunnel to tunnel. Then he saw light ahead with a figure standing there.

"We're going to make it!" He looked back, only to see MacAvoy being shot in the back by an arrow. It didn't matter; he had to make it, to change time.

He was closing in on the door; 16 seconds remained. He felt an arrow hit his leg and stumbled but kept running. The adrenaline in his body pumped as he ran limping. 8 . . .7 . . . 6 . . . He dove at the person in the opening, knocking her off balance. They fell out of the cave; 4 seconds remained. He noticed the scroll in her hand, grabbed it, took the dry matches from his pocket, lit it on fire, and threw the gold case in the tunnel as it closed up. He had destroyed the time warp.

"Well, hi. I'm Alicia Hawkins."

Brian Hughes :: Grade 7
Blake Middle School :: Hopkins

UNTITLED

When I hear
an electric guitar
I think of a car
screeching in the street,
and a bike skidding on my
driveway, and my sister
screaming in the bathroom.
The screeching sound of the
electric guitar makes my mom
go crazy, and makes me
fill with joy.

Justin Rubink :: Grade 3
Sand Creek Elementary School :: Coon Rapids

THE PIANO

My mom bought
me a piano
in the summer.
The keys are as shiny
as the sun in
the sky.
The color was as
colorful as a
rainbow playing with
the rain.
The notes are as
sharp as shark teeth in
the ocean.
The keys were as hard
as rock standing still on the
hill.
Playing the piano is
like walking in the air
in the sky
playing with Cupid.

Loan Hoang :: Grade 4
East Consolidated Elementary School :: St. Paul

THE ROCKET MAN (CHARACTER SKETCH)

The city air was hot and the August wind burned at
Rocket's face. His head was starting to get dizzy as he pedaled
faster and faster on his brand new 10 speed. As he picked up
speed with every passing moment, he and his bike became
nothing but a blur. Sometimes Rocket liked to ride this road
that led out of the ghettos and slums into the wealthier suburbs
of the city. He would imagine as he pedaled that he was leaving
these ghettos forever. The 10 speed was a Porsche and Rocket
was king. But these were only dizzying dreams that floated
through his mind as Rocket's legs pumped harder and harder
making his thigh muscles ripple like tiny waves upon the ocean.

The hill was approaching. It was the last part of his jour-
ney out of the slums. Once on top he could coast gently and si-
lently down into the parks and playlands of the rural folk.
Rocket's legs pumped like pistons generating more power to
start his ascent of the hill. Every muscle in his long but strong
legs were now being tested. They screamed at him to stop, but
Rocket moved on. They stretched and flowed so much, Rocket
was sure they would burst right through his skin. A few more
feet and he would be on top. His lungs were burning and his
heart raced, but Rocket made it. Once on top Rocket rolled
slowly to a stop. He stared down and faced the strange new
world that awaited him at the bottom of the hill. The smell of
roses and the green grass that covered the yards and parks
drifted lightly on the air. Rocket took deep breaths as he tried
to catch his wind. But he felt good. He gazed down at the
beautiful houses below. It seemed to him that every yard was its
own little world filled with beautiful flowers and trees. He often
thought that what was at the bottom of the hill was not the
suburbs at all but rather a wonderful painting that some artist
had masterfully created. Rocket stared mystified, almost en-
tranced. Then he shook his head and began his smooth coast
down.

Rocket loved this part of the city. Class—that was the
word here. Still, at home, amongst run down buildings, where

factory smoke stacks belched smog into the air; where cracked pavement covered the ground instead of grass; where the sky was grey instead of blue; Rocket was the man. Everybody knew Rocket. He was 6'5" and the best athlete the inner city had ever known. He did it all. He could run faster, jump higher and throw harder than anybody on both the East and West Sides. He was the Rocket Man. In the ghettos, kids idolized him, girls loved him, and even though some guys hated him, it was only out of jealousy. As he pedaled slowly around the suburbs he began to look around. Rocket saw many faces along the streets, and not one of them knew him. He kind of liked that. He didn't have to prove anything here, he could rest easy . . . for awhile.

Rocket had never known a world outside the slums. The inner city parks were where Rocket first made his name known. With his high flying rim shaking dunks and his sweet moves, it wasn't long before everybody knew his name. And Rocket loved the attention. He loved the domination, the power that he held wherever he went. Rocket loved being the best, in fact he lived for it. But he'd often wondered, would that all leave him when he left the city? The ghettos? Home? Would it all just disappear, all the greatness and power, once Rocket finally left the city behind? He'd seen some other guys play basketball from other cities and they were pretty good, which made Rocket worry.

Rocket dribbled towards the nearest hoop and began to shoot around. With the grace and beauty of a ballet dancer, Rocket sank shots effortlessly. Rocket loved the silence of the world as the ball slowly left his fingertips spinning and floating, drifting upwards towards the sky and then down through the net sounding like an ocean wave crashing on the rocks of the surf. Before he knew it, he was sweating and breathing heavy under the sweltering August heat. As his last shot drifted downwards and through the cords of the net a raindrop also fell. It fell upon Rocket's body that was now glistening with sweat. Then it began to rain a little harder and soon it was pouring as if every angel from the heavens above had started to weep.

Rocket took cover under the nearest tree, a towering oak that seemed to cut off the sky. It was here where Rocket watched the rain form puddles like so many lakes upon the court.

When the rain finally let up Rocket grabbed the ball and hopped on his bike. It was always slower going home, at least it seemed that way. But that's where he was going. Home. And as he once again began to climb the same hill that brought him into the suburbs he didn't seem to mind it as much as before. And as he neared the top he looked around and down into the ghettos that awaited him; the buildings no longer looked as bad as before and the sky wasn't as grey, and for a brief moment the ghettos seemed to smile at him. It was then, with the basketball still tucked tightly under his arm, that Rocket knew he was home. And maybe for now home wasn't such a bad place. It was where he was loved, where he grew up, and it was his for the taking. Here is where he was known. Here is where he was the Rocket Man.

Kurtis Sufka :: Grade 12
Royalton High School :: Royalton

My Dog

My dog
the obese canine
not eating to live
but living to eat
bred to be a sled dog
bred to be large
large she is
sled dog she's not
with arthritis
can barely move
the scary thing is
she's at her prime
only time can tell
the fate of this dog
my dog
the beached whale
with legs.

Jamie Jackish :: Grade 8
Twin Bluff Middle School :: Red Wing

JIM

Jim wears a red and blue striped scarf, bedroom slippers with holes in them, and has scratchy whiskers. His face is thin, covered with long, curly, white snarled hair. He sleeps between two trash cans on 7th Street in Saint Paul. For a pillow he uses a crumpled grocery bag. For a blanket he uses an old plastic bag. When Jim tosses and turns in his sleep, he wakes up all the alley cats. Then they start meowing and wake him up.

Jim is very sad inside, but strong also. He doesn't want anyone to know he's sad, so he acts crabby to cover it up. He gets his food from one of the two garbage cans. Jim's usual meal is a half eaten Big Mac and sour milk with leftover cold chicken.

Jim's hands are wrinkled and bitten by the cold. His lips are cracked and bleeding. He wears a red sweater with holes and paint stains all over it. He has a pair of bib overalls, which he throws over his thin, weak body, that he found in a garbage bag one day. One of Jim's socks is purple and the other is plaid. He wears an orange hat that is so small, it doesn't even cover his ears. Everything makes Jim feel small or alone. Even a group of ants make him feel lonely. He is afraid to face the city, where people stare at him and point. Jim wishes he was back with his job as a truck driver, and living in his warm house, instead of being here on the streets with no food or warmth.

One Saturday, at 3:00 in the afternoon, Jim decides to take a walk. Then he sees a sign as big as his alley that says: LANDMARK CENTER. He walks up the stairs and pulls the heavy glass doors open. Jim looks around at the marble walls and wooden floors. The place looks like a palace to him. He walks to a flight of stairs. Slowly, he crawls up seven flights. His old, worn out body can't climb up any further.

Jim comes to a hallway with rooms. One room is full of tables and cushioned chairs. Sunlight pours through the stained glass windows. Across from that room, he hears someone play soft music on a piano. Jim drags himself to a table and lies down. He slowly drifts off into another world. There are people all around him, respecting him, loving him. Jim wishes he would never wake up. When he does wake up, he feels lighter than ever, and he seems to be flying—up, up, into happiness.

Two weeks later, a gravestone stands in the cemetery with Jim's name on it. Few people came to his funeral.

Sarah Tollefson :: Grade 4
Carver Elementary :: Maplewood

FUTURE

i think of the summer
grandparents and cousins
new york and oceans
sitting by a campfire . . . listening
coyotes baying at the moon.
1990 shall be of peace
yet what's one year in
a future ahead?
writing is in my future
and our children will be us
one day.
yet now I only think . . .
. . . think of the summer

Barbara Van Sickle :: Grade 8
Princeton Middle School :: Princeton

IN ONE THOUSAND YEARS

I want to see
a bright, fuzzy bumble bee,
but who knows,
We may have a killer snow
In the next 1,000 years.

I want to feel
the skin of a seal,
Anyone else care?
They may evaporate into air,
In the next 1,000 years.

I want to know
If the spirit in all things
still shows,
I want it to soar
from shore to shore
for the next 1,000 years.

Tavanna Buske :: Grade 5
Jefferson Elementary School :: Rochester

LOVE WILL BUILD A WALL

The Construction Workers in My Heart

I used to believe construction workers lived in my stomach and would build houses and buildings there. They'd use my macaroni and cheese as logs and my milk as cement. They'd take my corn to use as bricks and they'd even take my suckers to use as big red trees. When a house or building was complete, I'd be full and want nothing else to eat. But now the construction workers are gone and there's an emptiness in my heart I can't explain.

Josh Moore :: Grade 5
Shirley Hills Elementary School :: Mound

Sister Love

When I'm laying in bed wide awake I can hear the wind
whistling to its buddies, my dad stomping through the
house complaining because Mom had to work late, thunder
crashing and lightning whipping through the trees. I
can also see my sister walking around crying. As I go
to the ladder to help her, I can feel the cold boards
crackle and my nightgown turned backwards. When I
get down to my sister I can almost taste the tears trickling
down her cheek. I can feel her little body rubbing up to
me for comfort. As my sister and I head up the ladder I can
feel the warmth and love of being a sister. When we get up
to my bed I can see her smiling inside of herself.

Lea Determan :: Grade 4
Holdingford Elementary School :: Holdingford

The Earthquake

Shaking!
Falling!
Wetness,
Tingly stomach feelings.
Divorce— Disgusting word,
Echoing
Louder and Louder!

Mom, Dad,
Swoop down,
Lift me up!
Change your mind.
I love you.

Stephanie Trossevin :: Grade 5
Glen Lake Elementary School :: Hopkins

FEAR

He walked out of my life at two
and came in and walked out at three.
Seven was when he came here and I
saw him last.
He walked out that time too.
I have the fear of never seeing him again.
At thirteen he sent a plane ticket so I could fly out.
A month I spent with him and all the time having
the fear of leaving.
I have the fear of him leaving my life for good.
I have the fear of him.

Rachel Firchow :: Grade 8
Central Middle School :: Columbia Heights

WHY?

Why is the boy sad?
Because the birds whispered of the long journey
of life ahead of him.

Why does it rain?
Because the broken hearted moon weeps for
the distant stars.

Why does the volcano erupt?
Because the anger trapped inside
escapes madly as it cries for air.

Why was the boy sad?
Because he was afraid of the
wonders of life.

John Slusarczyk :: Grade 8
Oltman Junior High School :: St. Paul Park

Uncle Harold, you were my cloud,
Holding in the rain.
You made the sun shine on my eyes
and on my golden hair.
You meant everything to me.
I wish I could tell you that,
but you've passed away.

The moments we had:
when you were hiding the matzah,
or telling me and Jennifer "Don't fight."

Now your cloud is gone,
now the rain is pouring against my cheeks
and my tears follow
as they drop onto the green grass.

Molli Mayeron :: Grade 3
Meadowbrook Elementary School :: Golden Valley

Chip and Lester (character sketch)

Lester is a crazy kid about 12 and he has a best friend named Chip. Chip got his nickname from eating Ruffles Potato Chips with burning hot jalapeno cheese. Lester and Chip are in a club named Dare Devils and they'll roll down a hill in an empty garbage can or jump off a gravel pit at the top point to the bottom. They joke around a lot. Lester is known for being weird, daring and sticking two tennis balls in his mouth. He lives in a house that is messy everywhere you look! Lumpy oatmeal laying on the black dappled counter and an old fish tank with no fish in it waiting to be cleaned. Chip knows how to make parents trust him. He says, "All you have to do is talk Lester into helping out in some of the household chores!" Lester's mom loves Chip, she'll let Chip do anything with Lester. Lester wears anything that's comfortable, even if it looks dumb. And Chip, on the other hand, well, he'll wear something that looks cool but is itchy all over. Some days, Lester is sad. When he doesn't even know what he is sad about. Chip has never seen Lester cry and Lester has never seen Chip cry. Chip and Lester will always be friends.

Cole Yetter :: Grade 5
Hillside Elementary School :: Cottage Grove

I Have Hands

Listen.
The sea, cries of gulls,
pitter-patter rain drops,
Beethoven and laughing children,
jackhammers and drills
and rumbling trains—all these you can hear.
But you cannot hear me.
I have no voice,
but I have hands
that speak for me.
I have many stories to tell,
many jokes to make,
many secrets to share . . .
but you don't care.
My foreign language
intrudes upon your daily noises
and you crawl farther
into your eggshell world.
I am human!
You enjoy tormenting me
with your endless stares,
making me feel worthless,
and all I can do
is sign: I love you . . .

Gail Mollner :: Grade 12
Cretin-Derham Hall High School :: St. Paul

SMALL, BIG HANDS

his hand tells a story alone
each indentation
each mark
holding a special event
the worn down skin
a sign of work
the marks on his thumb
beholding a war with no end
the mark where his ring finger had been
showing the truth of that war
then all at once
he woke up
a small boy
trapped
in a man's dream.

Eric Ruff :: Grade 7
LeSueur Junior High :: Le Sueur

HEAVY SPRING

Heavy Spring drapes me down
    Makes me want to die.
Every year I wonder if, you
    See what makes me cry.

It's all too good for me, you see,
    He laughs, I call it guilt.
It's all too sad for us to see.
    He smirks, I want to melt.

Heavy Spring drapes me down
    Makes me want to die.
Every year I wonder if, you
    See what makes me cry.

He loves me, he loves me not,
    Not today,
        It's way too hot.
Footsteps of Spring
    Come crashing in
        They make me feel weak,
        They make me feel thin.

Heavy Spring drapes me down
    Makes me want to die.
Every year I wonder if, you
    See what makes me cry.

Heavy Spring, full of flowers and sad
      Things.
    I want to cry
    I'll tell you why.
Because of Heavy Spring.

Samantha Loven :: Grade 10
Swanville Schools :: Swanville

UNTITLED

My brain is a bowling ball
in the bowling alley. My heart
is a pencil writing a
letter. My body is a hand
grenade setting our country
free. My stomach
is a chalk board waiting
to get written on.
My hands are spiders climbing
up their web.
My ears are seashells
waiting to get picked up.

Chase Davis :: Grade 1
Aquila Elementary School :: St. Louis Park

To My Past Teacher

I will never forget how much you hated me.
You never gave me a chance.
You never knew who I really was.
You had no right to tell me who I can and can't
    be friends with, you're not my mom.
You never let us do anything, not even dress up
    for Halloween.
I will never forget your wrinkling face, your hair
    that was turning gray, and that evil eye you
    gave everyone except XX.
Don't you have feelings?
Don't you like kids?
Or was it just me?
I don't see why you hated me,
I got good grades and I always
turned my work in on time.
Why? Why me?
I never did anything to you.

Heather Koch :: Grade 8
Central Middle School :: Columbia Heights

UNTITLED

Is my foot like my hand? Why? Or why not?
They are both on my body, I use them both,
but my hand has fingers, and my toes are on my foot.
One is on my leg, one is on my arm.
My foot looks like a manatee, the master of the water,
but my hand is like a bird, flying south
for the winter. My hand writes,
my foot walks. One holds a shoe, one holds chalk.
Could my foot be like grass on the bottom of the earth?
Could my hand be leaves on a tree high in the air?
They work together like a screw and a screwdriver.
When I shoot a basketball I can raise my hand high
like the Statue of Liberty and at the same time
my angry foot stomps down like Scrooge McDuck.
Sometimes my hand chases my foot
like a hungry fox after a helpless mouse.

Andy Leisen :: Grade 6
Southland Middle School :: Elkton

Untitled

Whenever I smell the fresh spring air it takes me back to 1980. I remember going outside when I came home from school, not wanting to come inside because of the baby. That's what she was called the first three months. The Baby. The baby needs this, the baby needs that. The baby was a helpless soldier, stranded without help. No one cared about me. I just stayed in the fresh spring air. I could just sit there, not caring about the baby, unlike my parents who thought she was a cute little bundle. I couldn't go inside for an hour, but if I did, who would know, who would care? Would it be like this forever? In that year the fresh spring air was my family. It woke me in the morning. It listened to me, not telling me to stay away from the baby because it might get a cold. My family, the fresh spring air.

Scott Bicking :: Grade 8
Shakopee Junior High School :: Shakopee

Untitled

CHARACTERS: DR. MAGGOT (Head Surgeon), CHUCK JONES (Morgue owner), DR. ZINK (Assistant), YOUNG GIRL, MANY EXTRAS

PLACE: Dark, dimly lit room. Painted dark red. Room is completely empty except for a tall glass table in the room. On the table is a female heart.

TIME: Night, about 8:00 p.m.

(*DR. MAGGOT* AND *DR. ZINK* ENTER THE ROOM IN WHITE LAB COATS. THEY WALK DIRECTLY TO THE HEART)

DR. MAGGOT
Well, Zink, it looks like her heart is forever broken.

DR. ZINK (POKING & PRODDING HEART)
Yeah, it looks that way to me too. I wonder what happened.

DR. MAGGOT (PUZZLED)
It looks like the cause was (GENTLY POKES THE HEART) maybe a male species?

DR. ZINK
I just saw a broken heart with the identical looks. That's got to be it, or something of the sort.

DR. MAGGOT
So should we conclude the autopsy as causally male?

DR. MAGGOT & DR. ZINK (LOOK AT EACH OTHER, NOD)
(TOGETHER)
Most definitely.

SCENE II. TWO WEEKS LATER.

CHUCK JONES (UPSET)
Well, Dr. Maggot, I can't keep this here forever. Someone has got to claim it. Two weeks is over policy! You know that!

DR. MAGGOT (DISTURBED)
I realize that, Mr. Jones. But there is some poor girl out there with a broken heart. You just don't understand the importance of this!

CHUCK JONES (SARCASTICALLY)
No, obviously not.

DR. ZINK (PICKING UP HEART)
Well, someone's heart broke approximately three weeks ago. If we don't find her, I will never rest in peace.

DR. MAGGOT
Ditto. Now let's find her!

(THERE IS AN ANGRY SILENCE IN THE ROOM *CHUCK* WALKS OVER TO THE HEART, PICKS IT UP AND HOLDS IT OVER THE GARBAGE. JUST AS HE IS ABOUT TO THROW IT AWAY, A *YOUNG GIRL* WALKS IN TIMIDLY)

YOUNG GIRL
Hi, um, by any chance do you have a broken heart you found two weeks ago?

DR. MAGGOT & DR. ZINK (IN UNISON)
By George! We've found her!

SCENE III.

(*DR. ZINK* AND *DR. MAGGOT* ARE SMOKING CIGARS AT THE LOCAL BAR)

DR. ZINK
Did you see the look on her face when we asked her the cause?

DR. MAGGOT (LAUGHING)
Oh, yeah, she looked sufficiently embarrassed if I do say so my-self. She never answered us, did she?

DR. ZINK (SMILING TO HIMSELF)
Nope. But when I asked her if a male was the cause, her jaw dropped and she said, "How did—?" I guess she never really finished.

DR. MAGGOT (HESITANTLY)
So it is safe to conclude it was an involuntary action of the male species?

DR. ZINK (SMUGLY)
You bet!

Michele Webb :: Grade 10
Richfield High School :: Richfield

SADNESS COMING

My mom is jolly even though
she's thin and then her smile turns
upside down. I look at her
face. Something forces me
to ask her the astonishing
question. My mom gives
me a dress, trying to keep
tears off of her face.
I look at it, wondering
what I shall think. Then
my dad takes me
somewhere and I realize
an orphanage. I felt angry,
sad, discouraged, felt like ripping
my red dress. And now,
I look it over and start in
crying and say why
didn't my mom say
good-bye?

Lucimara Harmon :: Grade 5
Central Elementary :: Bemidji

EYES

Eyes . . .
    Twittering, adjusting
    always moving
    a constant whirling
    grandfather clock
    pulsing — then resting

Eyes . . .
    Opening — shutting
    a shutter
    on an old rickety windowpane
    mounted on an 18th century house
    fluttering in the wind

Eyes . . .
    Focusing, panning
    searching for something —
    but always slightly out of reach
    maybe a treasure or
    invitation to love
    buried in the coldness of eternity.

Eyes . . .
    Looking towards the future
    our window to the outside,
    we plead for "out"
    a pleasant alternative —
    a treasure in itself.

Benjamin Horn :: Grade 6
Richfield Intermediate School :: Richfield

"He eats with his mouth open!" yelled Squirrely and Whirly the squirrels. "He picks his nose while he's eating!" They yelled again.

"I do not!" screamed Herman the koala. "I do not!" he screamed again.

"Oh gross!" Shena cried as she ran out the door. Shena was Herman's girlfriend, but since Squirrely and Whirly had said that stuff about Herman she didn't want to be his girlfriend.

Herman had a problem. He had girlfriends, but then when he got close to them the squirrels would take over and Herman would never see them again. "Why do you do this to me?" Herman shouted.

"We don't like your turquoise Hawaiian flowered bowtie or your checkered pants and suspenders," they said.

"Is that all?!"

"We don't like you either I guess," said Whirly.

They shouted back and forth for days. Then Herman called Rhonda and asked her out. Rhonda had heard that he was messy and many other things. He called Sue, Anne, Crystal, and soon he had called everyone. They had all heard about his dark side. Then when he was dancing for the Monkeysons' granny's one hundredth birthday party he tripped on a toy and broke his leg.

"Oh no! I'll never have a wife now," Herman cried.

A week later his nurse was bringing him to his treehouse from a walk and they were talking. She noted the seed collection and the nut collection.

"I live with two squirrels who tell all my girlfriends about my dark side," he said.

"Well I'm very messy and kind of gross sometimes. I can't find a husband," she said.

"Neither can I, well, a wife I mean," Herman said.

That day Herman found a wife, and no matter what anyone said she still loved him.

Kaisie Melom :: Grade 6
Bamber Valley Elementary School :: Rochester

WHY?

Why do we love?
Because we need water to cure
the drought of life.

Why do hearts get broken?
Because the heavens' peace was
overtaken by lightning.

Why do we marry?
Because the hands of death
need cuffs.

Why do we cheat?
Because we find more, somewhere
over the rainbow.

Why do we lie?
Because our hearts are too heavy to
stand alone.

Why do we divorce?
Because we feel the lock from the coffin
has been broken.

Why do we love?

Tawnya Essen :: Grade 8
Oltman Junior High School :: St. Paul Park

THE DAY OF A *STRESSFUL* MAN

I was downhill skiing down this huge mountain. I stopped to take a look in the woods. I took off my skis and started walking. Kelli was down on this bridge with a fishing rod and she was fishing with a bare hook. She got it caught in her sweater and beckoned me to help her get it out. I don't have any idea how to get it out I said. Why not she whined. It's because I'm having a hard time thinking of anything to write about. Well you're pretty dumb. It's not that I'm dumb it's that this story is dumb and I can't be creative over something I dislike. So then she slapped me. Kelli, I said Don't get Mad if I like blow you up or something, remember it's only a story. She told me she understood. All of a sudden the teenage mutant ninja turtles came out of nowhere and started breakdancing on the bridge. Great Joe now this story is just so much better Kelli commented, I'm mad at you, you're made at yourself and the turtles are mad that there hasn't been a "raps greatest hits" cd out in a while, boy oh boy this is bound to get published. Fine fine I've started off poorly and I've gotten worse but you're not exactly helping either. Oh ok Joe point fingers you spineless wimp. That's it I'm done I have nothing else to write about. "JOE!" Suddenly a commanding voice sounded from the top of the mountain. Fix this story or die Joe . . . But with what shall I fix dear Henry dear — Joe Knock It off — Now I want you to fix the story and do it right. ah hem

I could feel the wind fly past my ears. My heart was pumping I was skiing down Pikes Peak at speeds never thought reachable. Suddenly I stopped I saw the one thing that holds meaning in my life, my girlfriend Kelli. She was casting a hook into the quiet stream below the bridge she stood on. I came down to greet her when the Russians dropped an atomic bomb and we all died.

There, how's that oh wise voice here is my story I hope thou ist pleasedth with thine hardeth worketh.

"You should add more to it Joe it kind of lacks content." Well Hey I will if I had time but it's the weekend now and my brain is shutting off until Monday. I understand Joe I'm going to let go of your responsibilities. Thank you oh wise voice, you know how bad I need a break. Yes I do Joe until Monday. I will hear you Monday.

The skies then cleared and I walked home whistling.

Joe Albrecht :: Grade 12
Elk River High School :: Elk River

UNTITLED

A woman
carries a bag
and watches her feet
as she walks.
Broken dreams
weigh down her shoulders
with sad
down-turned eyes
she shuffles on,
out of sight.

A man walks aimlessly.
He sends
darting glances
around him.
He steps carefully
as if
he doesn't want to bother
the rest
of the world.

This neighborhood
is just a shell
lying in tribute
to what life
has become
to them.

Erin Lloyd :: Grade 9
Richfield Junior High School :: Richfield

LOVE WILL BUILD A WALL

The people's heart is filled with gold.
We hope that one day people will sing
together and love together. Hero's thoughts
are glued with power. One man can
do anything. Life has many joys,
a Rabbit in a hat or a famous person
touching us. We can make a
difference. The wind will cry with
the sound of rain. The world will
be happy again. People's love will
build a wall that will
keep out hate. The world will be
happy again.

Tom Coon :: Grade 5
Katherine Curren Elementary School :: Hopkins

My Name's Rescue

THE GREAT POOL ADVENTURE

Hi! My name is Willy. I'm a *cute* Yorkshire with a grey body which grows lighter as it gets to my head. My head is light tan and white. I have two friends, Butch, the Chihuahua and Pierre, the tabby cat. Since I'm much cuter than them, you probably wouldn't want to hear about them. The three of us live in Lakeland, Minnesota, in a little one-storey house with lots of flowers and plants. This is where my story takes place.

It was a very hot summer day. Mr. and Mrs. Sill, our owners, were getting up. I don't mind them getting up, but at 6:30 in the morning! On Summer Vacation! The only thing that's okay with that is that Butch, Pierre and I get our Science Diet earlier. We were eating our food when I heard Mrs. Sill say, "What are you going to do today?"

"Probably bring Will in for a hair cut and then set up that pool for Tim and Sam," Mr. Sill said. Oops! I forgot to tell you about Tim and Sam. They are the sons of the Sills. Tim and Sam are twins so I never really know who I greet at the door. Like their parents, they are tall and have dark hair and dark eyes. Back to our story.

Now, when I heard that I was getting a hair cut I wanted to disappear. But Mr. Sill mentioned a pool! What was a pool? I didn't have time to think because Mr. Sill had swept me up and started to carry me to the car.

When I got back, I felt exhausted. But my exhaustion disappeared when Butch came running and said, "There's a huge plastic monster out there. You can hear it sloshing its insides. What are we going to do?" During that time Butch was running around in circles. I got so dizzy that I fell.

We ran outside as soon as I got up and saw Pierre running toward us. His fur was soaking wet and smelled queer. "I was attacked! I shoved the Monster and it practically drowned me in water! Hey, Willy, what happened to your hair?"

"Don't even ask. Come on, we've got to stop this thing before it attacks Mr. and Mrs. Sill." Running outside, we came upon the monster. I tore off a piece of it and the next thing I knew, I was being drowned in cold water! Mr. and Mrs. Sill came running out and picked me up.

"Willy don't worry! It's only a pool!" Mrs. Sill picked up Butch and Pierre. They were soaked too. We were brought inside and dried off.

I heard Mr. Sill grumble, "I've got to get a new pool now." Maybe next year I will know what a pool is. Hey! Anything could happen!

Michelle Lee :: Grade 5
Woodbury Middle School :: Woodbury

The Dog and the Frosty Day

The brown and white dog lingers around.
He is looking for a nice fat bird to chase.
The brown and white dog lingers around
looking at many things. He feels the frosty
air blow by his fur, making a sound like
a ghost, whoooooo. The brown and white dog
lingers around looking at many things.
The sound of dead crisp leaves being
raked into big piles. Then children come
out and jump into the frosty leaves.
The brown and white dog lingers around
He sees the boy who is always
biking or playing football at all
temperatures then comes into his
house with his face tomato red.
The brown and white dog lingers around
then itches himself and looks at himself
in a mirror of water and sees an image
of a dog who looks like a chocolate sundae.

Anita Kumar :: Grade 3
Bamber Valley Elementary :: Rochester

"Why can't I live as a normal person?" asked Don. "I think I'll take a jog through the mine field to town," he said.

As Don is running through the mine field he realizes there are no big booms behind him.

"Those dumb bombs never go off!" Don yells. "Well, I have no time to fix them now," he thinks.

Now Don is in town and he walks into the local market.

"Hi, I would like two dozen eggs and a pound of ham. Eh, how much will this be?" Don asks.

"Three fifty-one," says the lady at the counter.

"O.K. Oops! I forgot my wallet!" shrieks Don. "I'll be back in a minute!" he says, running out of the store.

While Don is running home, he is talking to himself. "I can't do anything right," he says,.

THUMP!

"Oww! I'm gonna rip that stump outa the ground!" yells Don holding his foot. He finally hobbles to his cabin and back to the store. "There's your dumb three fifty-one," Don says. "Now I'll go to the restaurant and have some lunch," he says to himself.

Now Don wobbles over to the restaurant where they are having a contest. For the millionth customer: a house right in town and free breakfast for one year. Don opened the door and . . .

BONG!

"What the . . ." Don says.

"Sir, you're the millionth customer here. You win a free house and breakfast for one year," says the owner.

Don says, "I can't believe this! I've never won anything in my life!"

"Well, you believe it," said the owner.

So Don lived and ate in peace with the rest of the towns-people.

Daniel Nielsen :: Grade 6
Sandstone Elementary School :: Sandstone

DETECTIVE SNUGGLEBUG

My name is Snugglebug. I'm a private eye. I'm white, black, and orange. I'm a cat and I'm curious. My eyes are aqua blue and I have a very long tail. I have big feet, a tan trench coat and I live in a big doll house. In the morning I get up, get dressed, make my bed, comb my whiskers, brush my teeth. Then I eat a frozen mouse and a glass of water. But my dream is that I had one hundred mice to feast on. But I can't get any money because I never have any cases to solve. After I had just finished breakfast I went into the living room and picked up the newspaper and saw a reward. It read: *Reward* two *tons* of mice *if* a nosy cat is found. I just threw down the paper and got on my trench coat and headed toward the door. And when I got outside I saw the nosy cat! He was running away from the police. Then I told the police that I will go after the crook. They said I could!

Jamie Kreuser :: Grade 3
New Prague Elementary School :: New Prague

My Name

My name is as white as a mourning dove

My name is a mourning dove singing
a dusky song, like the twilight
wind in the moony sky, like a marigold
shining silver, like flames of fire
shining at night, light a blizzard flowing
out moon shreds.

Gary Bogatz :: Grade 3
Detroit Lakes Elementary School :: Detroit Lakes

MIRROR, MIRROR

Carl Thorton sat watching the young couple kissing on one of the newer graves, before an immaculate tombstone; behind them a gentle breeze began stirring the bare branches of one of the maples. They were in their teens, as he'd imagined them, and the boy had just begun unbuttoning the girl's blouse when the skeletal hand reached up out of the earth and grabbed the girl's ankle.

She screamed, of course, before she even knew what had grabbed her, but when she looked down and saw the bones wrapping her leg, the arm connected to those fingers, the whole rotting corpse rising from the ground, she screamed even harder. Its face was the unearthly white of a full moon in Los Angeles, and as wrinkled as a desiccated apple; shreds of skin fluttered from its cheeks. On its head was a cap of black matted hair, and rotting teeth hung in its putrid face as it opened its mouth to eat.

The boy yanked the girl to her feet and pulled her out of the zombie's grip; he was bellowing now also, like a steer being led to a slaughter. The two of them bolted for the graveyard's gate but the earth beneath them began to churn. It split open before them and from the rent graves three more bodies rose, with outstretched arms and open mouths . . .

Very nice effects, very nice indeed, Thorton thought as the house lights came back on; the audience giggled and groaned and applauded as Dick Cavett smirked to show how silly he thought the whole horror book/movie phenomenon was. God! Thorton thought, how he hated these wretched publicity tours, how he hated, in fact, every one of those fans out there who had made him the world's best selling horror novelist. Why did people have to have faces and hands that wanted to touch you and questions and . . .

"We're here with Carl Thorton," Dick Cavett intoned. "The author of *Screamdreams*, as well as, among others, *Decomposing Bodies* and *Attack of the Grizzlies*. Now that was an interesting clip, Carl. Some members of our audience seemed offended by that scene while others thought it was funny. And you're smiling, as if you enjoyed their reaction."

"I DID enjoy it, Dick," Thorton said. "Movies like that should make an audience react. If they just sat there, I'd be worried."

"So it doesn't matter if people don't like your movie . . . "

"I wrote the book, Dick," Thorton reminded him, "not the movie. But I don't write to be LIKED, if that's what you mean. I write because I . . . I write because I . . . I don't know why I write."

"To make money?" Cavett asked, and the audience laughed.

"That too," Thorton conceded.

"So tell me your honest opinion of the film. Did it do your book justice? I mean, you're the REAL star of the picture; your name is what will bring people to the theater."

"I like things in it, Dick," Carl explained. If he could just get through this last interview, the publicity tour would be over; how many times would he have to answer the same question? "I like the zombies we just saw. There's a chainsaw killing that's very effective, and another scene in which a hooded strangler creeps up behind the girl. That's terrifying, I think."

Then Cavett asked a question Thorton couldn't answer. "Where do all these horrors come from? These mutilations and grotesqueries. You think them up, of course, and they've made you rich. But do you have nightmares? Are these phantasms somehow a mirror of you, the man?"

"Do I look like a ghoul?" Carl Thorton said and smiled. The audience hooted and whistled, loving it. For Thorton, at thirty-nine, could have been an idol. He was tall, slim, impeccably groomed and expensively dressed; he was charming, seductive, adroit in conversation. He was recently divorced, a big news item in the ENQUIRER and the STAR. And he knew he figured quite prominently in the dreams of his female fans. With his close-up on the back of the jacket of every book, he knew he scared them with the text, then soothed them to sleep with his picture. But where DID those horrors come from?

A studio limousine was waiting at curbside, and he jumped in the back, slammed the door quickly and sank back in the rich upholstery.

The driver immediately stepped on the gas; it was over— Carl Thorton was going home. They drove several miles through the downtown traffic in perfect silence, but as the chauffeur entered the winding residential area where Carl Thorton lived, he cleared his throat and said, "A very good show, Mr. Thorton."

"Thanks very much," Carl said, and hoped he could leave it at that.

"Don't those creepy stories give you the willies?" the driver asked. "They sure give me the heebie jeebies."

"I don't get scared by that stuff," Thorton said. "But as long as other people do, I'll keep churning it out. You don't really believe in vampires, zombies, monsters—you just like to be frightened. It's the real stuff that scares me; talk show hosts, press agents, ex-wives, alimony payments, people who ask questions."

That shut him up. The driver didn't say anything until he drew up under the portico of Thorton's expensive house. "Here we are sir," the driver said. Thorton could tell he'd lost a fan.

"Thanks," he said. "God, do I hate publicity tours." He handed the driver a twenty to ease his conscience, grabbed his small bag, and hurried up the series of long slanted granite steps to the front door. A body was huddled on the welcome mat, and Thorton grunted in surprise. The noise woke the body; it was a kid, disheveled and pimply; a gawky, ugly kid who stood up nervously clutching a book and a manila envelope.

"What the hell are you doing on my doorstep?" Thorton yelled. His heart was pounding; the kid had startled him.

The kid began stuttering in an agony of embarrassment. "I . . . I . . . I'm sorry, Mr. Thorton, but would you, uh like, would you . . ." He thrust a copy of Thorton's latest novel SCREAMDREAMS at him. "Sign my book?"

"No I won't sign your book. You're trespassing on my property. This is my home. Get out of here!"

"But I'm, like, I'm you're biggest fan in the world. I've got all your books, every edition, hardcover and paperback and . . ." He shoved the book toward Thorton and the envelope spilled from the crook of his arm, pages littering the ground at his feet.

"And you're a writer and you'd like me to read your stuff right? I don't do business at home, kid." He looked with distaste at the trembling figure, the papers scrawled with cursive. "But here's a little advice. Learn to type." He opened the door with his key and slammed it behind him. The noise echoed in the amplitude of his pristine living room.

He grabbed the mail which lay in a pile at his feet, slung his bag over his shoulder, and started up the curved stairs to the second floor. As he walked, he sorted, letting the advertising circulars, the bills, the fan mail, fall at his feet. Greta, his housekeeper, had done her job well, as usual. The carpet still held the vacuum cleaner's strokes. French roses gleamed in a vase on the glass coffee table below him, and the calm pink walls radiated peace and warmth.

In the bedroom Thorton undressed hurriedly, flung open the louvered doors, and entered the bathroom, a huge space with mirrors on half the walls and an oval sunken marble tub. He turned the faucets on full, squeezed some bath gel into the rushing water and as steam drifted lazily upwards, he confronted himself in the mirror. His eyes were bloodshot and his skin looked slack. He stretched his cheeks until they were taut again. "You look pooped," he said. Then he pivoted, admiring the taut muscles of his abdomen, and slapped his stomach with his palm. "Pretty good for a writer," he said, and winked at himself.

The water was hot, as he liked it, and he sank beneath the surface bubbles until only his head rested on the rim of the marble tub. With his toes he reached up and shut off the pounding water. In the gleaming chrome, he thought he caught a flash of movement and he shipped his head around, but there was nothing there. Calm down, Carl, he thought as he allowed himself to sink completely under water, blowing bubbles, letting the warmth of the water drain the tension from his body.

He soaked a few minutes, then stood; he wrapped himself in a huge terrycloth towel and went to the sink under the mirror, now completely clouded with steam, to brush his teeth. With his hand, he wiped a swath of moisture away and in the small mirrored space saw his own face. And behind him, across the room, another face—grim, white, barely discernible.

Carl gasped and spun around. He was alone in his room. Across from him were the double French windows that looked out over his estate. He grinned, amazed at how tired he was, so tired he was seeing things, and turned back to the mirror.

He opened his mouth to brush his teeth and saw the face again. It was like the face of the zombie in the movie clip, dissolving even as he watched. Its body was visible now as it began climbing through the window.

Thorton yelled and turned around, his heart pounding in his throat. He was suddenly very angry. That goddamn kid, he thought. If it was him, he'd have the police here so fast . . . He strode to the windows, flung them open, and screamed, "Get out of here, you creep. If I catch sight of you again, I'll call the police . . ."

But there was no one in the garden below.

In the clear night sky, the moon hung oblivious to human error. He shut the windows with a bang, pulled the drapes, and stalked across the room toward the bedroom beyond. As he went, he couldn't keep his eyes from searching the mirror, and in it he saw the figure moving toward him.

He dropped the towel and ran naked and yelling into the bedroom, slamming the louvered doors behind him, snapping the latch. He put on his terrycloth robe and sat on the edge of the wide bed, shivering. What was going on? He'd never had waking dreams before. Sure, he'd had nightmares . . . everyone had them. But never like this, never when he was awake. He stared at the louvered doors, as though he expected a solemn knocking.

But the night was totally quiet; he strained to hear the noise of a car, a barking dog, anything. All he heard was the blood pounding in his temples. Was he going crazy? Could he be that tired?

He reached for the phone on the nightstand and quickly punched the seven digits of Kathy's number. They'd just begun seeing each other, and she wasn't committed to him, but if she were home, he'd ask her . . .

"Hello," Kathy's sultry voice said.

"Kathy, it's me," Thorton said. "Carl. Can you come over? I need—"

"This is Kathy," her voice said. "I can't come to the phone right now, but please, PLEASE don't hang up. Leave a message and let me know I didn't waste two hundred dollars on this machine. Thank you." The machine beeped, and the tape began rolling.

"It's Carl," Thorton said. "I've missed you. Please call as soon as you can." He hung up, and sat there breathing hard, hoping he didn't sound too hysterical. Women, he'd learned, don't like hysterical men.

He had to get a grip; there was nothing wrong. He stood, took a deep breath, and walked to the louvered doors, unlatched them and looked inside.

The bath was still full; the bubbles slowly disappearing. The room was empty, totally empty, except for the towel he'd discarded as he fled to the bedroom. He closed the doors again and latched them, and hurried downstairs to his den where he kept the liquor.

It was a spacious, well-lighted room, and Thorton hit every switch. His IBM PC was centered on a large mahogany table; two of the walls were lined with bookshelves, one entire shelf holding the collected works of Carl Thorton. The other walls held framed posters—WIVES FOR DINNER, HAITIAN ZOMBIE HONEYMOON—of the movies made from his books. He sat down in his leather chair and tried to keep his knees from shaking.

But it was no use. He stood, took a deep breath and

walked to the bar, where he poured himself a tumbler of Stolichnaya and drank it down straight. Almost immediately his hands stopped trembling. He poured another drink, and as he raised it to his lips, he looked into the mirror behind the bar.

Behind him stood a hooded man, clad entirely in black. His face was white and scabrous and covered in part by a skin-tight leather mask. He wore black gloves and held something in his hands . . .

Carl Thorton screamed and dropped the tumbler; he grabbed an ice pick from the bar and whirled to meet his attacker, but there was nothing behind him, just the den in which he'd written his books, the solid expensive furniture, the rich wine-colored carpet. He turned toward the mirror again and the hooded figure was there, so close he thought he saw black pools of absence where the eyes should have been. In rage and fear he grabbed the Stolichnaya and flung it at the mirror. The bottle burst, spraying vodka everywhere. And the mirror shattered.

But in every shard, Thorton saw a reflection of the hooded figure coming toward him, dozens of them raising their hands at him. He whirled around to find nothing behind him. "Give me a fugging break!" he screamed and stalked out of the den, slamming the door behind him.

He bolted every door in the house, shut and locked every window, pulled every drape. He tried Kathy again, but her recorded voice was no help. He huddled at the top of the stairs with nothing before or behind but carpeting; a loaded pistol lay on the step beside him. He held the hall phone on his lap and punched the seven digits of the L.A.P.D. "You have reached the Police Department," the computer voice informed him, "All of our lines are busy, please hold. All calls are being answered in order." Thorton looked at the clock on the wall. It was 12:01. He was still holding at 3:27 when he fell into exhausted sleep.

He awoke at 9:30 to the monotonous beep of a phone left off the hook, feeling foolish, wretched, still exhausted. He showered, shaved, dressed and opened every room in the house looking for some reason for his foolishness the night before. How could he have been so frightened? How could he have imagined a figure stalking him? Thorton tried to remember if he'd ever been so terrified, and remembered a recurring dream he'd had as a child, a dream in which his parents stood by solidly as he screamed for help, as a . . .

He wiped the memory from his mind. He thought of his fans with more disdain than ever; why would someone enjoy being frightened? Why would someone pay good money . . .

The den was in shambles, but as he pulled the drapes and sunlight flooded the room, he was relieved to find there was nothing there but what he, Carl Thorton, had bought and put there. He stayed away from the bar; Greta would clean it up.

Outside it was brilliant and clear. The smog was totally gone, and the sky was a deep cerulean. Azaleas, hydrangeas, rhododendrons were in bloom and their sweet smells drifted through the air as he drove toward Century City for a meeting with the executive producer of SCREAMDREAMS.

He drove the car up to the gatehouse, where he stopped in line to get his ticket. He was a little late, impatient, and ready to get on with the business of being a millionaire, a hot property, an adult.

The guy in front of him was asking the guard about something and Carl hit the horn once. Behind him he heard the sound of another car rolling to a stop, and the driver of that car, also impatient, leaning on his horn.

Thorton stole a glance in the rearview mirror, curious. Maybe he knew the driver. But all he saw was the leather-clad face of his attacker coming at him from the back seat. In his black gloved hands he held a strangler's cord.

Carl screamed, flung open the door, and bolted from the driver's seat. The security guard looked up from talking, and another guard standing idly by moved toward him. On his hip was a holster.

Carl ran to the man and grabbed his arms.

"Sir," the man said, "Your car . . ."

"He's trying to kill me," Carl yelled. "He wanted to strangle me!" He shook the man trying to get him to understand.

"What?" the man said. "Sir, your car."

Carl released the man and turned around. He didn't know the driver of the car behind his, but now the man was shaking a fist at him. "You have to move your car," the guard said. "You can't just leave it sitting there."

Carl took a deep breath and turned back toward the man. "I'm telling you, someone is trying to kill me!"

In the guard's mirrored glasses he saw the hooded figure raise the cord. Carl screamed and hit the man as hard as he could. The guard staggered backwards; his glasses flew from his face to the asphalt. With the heel of his shoe, Carl Thorton ground the glasses to powder as the guard drew his gun and told him to put his hands up.

He had never been in jail and found the experience less than pleasant. He felt more and more as if he was spiraling into a nightmare. Wait till the tabloids got ahold of this. MONSTER MAVEN ARRESTED FOR FREAKY DREAMS; MURDER EVERYWHERE, SAYS CARL THORTON.

He was grunting like a cornered animal when the attendant finally came with Kathy. For some reason she thought the whole thing was funny. "I can't take you anywhere," she said.

"Just get me out of here," he said, and let her take his hand and drag him out of jail.

They were zipping along Mulholland Drive in Kathy's Karmmann Ghia, and he was ashamed and embarrassed, but nothing she said could dissuade him of what he'd experienced.

"Home or office," she said as blithely as she could manage.

"Home, I guess," he said. Even he could tell how broken his voice sounded.

Somehow she managed to get him upstairs. First she blind-folded him, then she monitored each step he took, until she'd locked the bedroom door behind her, latched the louvered doors to the bathroom, undressed him and got him under the covers. He was shaking uncontrollably; he knew he'd lost his mind.

"Water," he said.

She brought him a glass of water and told him to close his eyes. Then she gently sat him up and brought the water to his lips; cool beautiful water in which he knew he could see his own reflection. He clamped his eyes down so hard it hurt.

"Pills," she said. "Open your mouth; I want you to take these pills." He did as he was told.

"Now lie back," she said. "And rest. This will help you sleep. And tomorrow we're going to see a doctor." There it was, what he'd been expecting all afternoon. Who could blame her?

How had he gotten to this state? He was the one who frightened people, not the one who gets frightened. They'd made him do it, they'd pushed him to this, his fans with their distorted faces and grabbing hands. His voracious, lascivious fans.

He turned to face her, "I'm sorry about all this. I . . . ."

"Shhhhhh," she said and put a finger to his lips. And then she moved to kiss him. He closed his eyes, felt the warmth and tender pressure of her lips. For the first time since he'd been in jail, he felt half-way human.

She pulled back and he took a deep breath, feeling the tension drain from him.

"Go to sleep," she said. "Everything will be fine tomorrow."

"I know," he said. He opened his eyes to look at her; she was very close, so close he could see his own reflection in her iris, and behind him, coming out of the bed itself, two black gloved hands slipped the garrote around his neck.

He was choking to death; he couldn't scream. Both his hands tried to pull the invisible cord away from his neck so he could get a breath, but the force was inhuman. He lunged upwards, but was pulled back. He thrashed on the bed in a paroxysm of terror and pain, as though he were being electrocuted.

Kathy was on her knees, screaming. "Carl!" she yelled. "God, Carl let me help you!"

And then the pressure ceased. He looked at Kathy; her hands covered her mouth and her eyes were wide with horror. He put his hands to his face and felt peeling skin, a black leather face mask, the flopping folds of a black hood.

"Noooo!" he screamed, tearing at his face. Kathy was shrieking now, wild hysterical shrieks that sounded like a police siren.

Carl Thorton bashed through the locked louvered doors into the bathroom. He ran to the mirror, but he knew what he would find. From somewhere he heard what sounded like laughter, applause, the tumultuous acclaim of a vast audience. His face was hideous, the unearthly white of a full moon in Los Angeles, and as wrinkled as a desiccated apple; shreds of skin fluttered from his cheeks. The face mask couldn't obscure who he was, and the black hood only worsened his pallor.

Kathy was slumped against the louvered doors, screaming in terror. He turned to the French windows, through which the sounds of wild applause were filtering. He gathered his strength and ran across the room, throwing himself through the window, into the arms of his invisible and adoring fans.

Matt Hansen :: Grade 11
Bemidji Senior High School :: Bemidji

MY NAME

My name is like a big white cloud
floating in the sky.
It is the American flag
waving in the wind.
My name is the soft green grass
that people like to lay on.
It is a student
sitting quietly in his seat.
But my last name is
like a wild animal going to the bathroom
in the woods.
It is like a deer
running from a cheetah
and getting eaten.
My last name is
a big black cloud, raining
and thundering and lightning
on all the people.
My last name is a naughty kid
who never does his work.

Wesley Misquadace :: Grade 7
McGregor Schools :: McGregor

UNTITLED

My mind
is like a Venus Fly Trap
because it is always grabbing for more information.
My legs are like big cranes
because they are big and powerful.
My heart is like
a volcano full of lava
because it is hot and steamy.
My arms are like a bear's claws.
They are big, strong and very powerful.
My blood is like a fire
because it is red and always burning like
wild fire.
My eyes are as hot and bright
as the sun.
My body is like the earth
because it is always on the move.

Daniel Carlson :: Grade 4
East Consolidated Elementary School :: St. Paul

"I guess you could say that I'm trapped in a dead end job."

Just to be sure, I had to ask, "Isn't there anyone who can benefit from your job?"

"In a tiny fragment of a way, I guess. But very little," Marvin replied disappointedly.

Up in the early morning, Marvin forces himself out of bed. Looking through his selection of clothes, Marvin throws on an old t-shirt and a comfortable pair of jeans. Marvin gets in his station wagon and drives to his daily destination, his workplace. Once there, Marvin immediately begins a typical work day. Two tons of three-foot high bottles await him. Lifting the bottles over his shoulders and under his arms, Marvin puts the fifty-pound bottles onto the cold, steel back of the truck, one by one. Reaching all corners of the Twin Cities, Marvin delivers purified water to some of the many customers his company has. "Sounds easy to me," I added.

"Of course not. I have stress just like any other job would. Bottles being carried to and from the truck isn't exactly easy. Strength is a much needed skill. You can't get too far without it," Marvin explained. Rounding to the back door, going to the front, going out the back door or wherever the customer prefers, the fifty pound bottles can be hard on your back, strong or not. Anything else? Definitely. Schedule. Schedule is very critical in a job like this. Marvin has to deliver to a city he is unfamiliar with. Traveling around side streets and unknown dirt roads, Marvin finds himself hopelessly lost. Taking occasional glances at his watch, Marvin realizes he is way off schedule. Not giving up, however, Marvin eventually finds where he is supposed to deliver with the help of road maps and gas station attendants. By this time of course, Marvin is an hour behind. An hour behind is three or four customers behind. An hour behind is also a little session of grief from the boss. Bosses, foreign cities, schedules, heavy loads . . . Is there anything Marvin could get or give out of this?

"Even though this isn't a job I could benefit from, others

tend to benefit from it. Oh yeah, and I guess I have more knowledge of the Cities now than I ever would have."

As Marvin gains knowledge of the Twin Cities, people await their purified water from their trusty waterman.

"So, I suppose if I wanted to make it sound as good as I could make it, I guess I would say I'm supporting health by delivering clean water. That's about the most people get out of my job," Marvin said honestly.

Growing up in a well-to-do Jewish family, Marvin was not destined to be a waterman. Marvin feels he was basically a victim of laziness which took him over and let him be subject to unsuccessful occupations. What had Marvin wished for? A penthouse overlooking the city and all of its problems, with none of his own.

"I regret the laziness, and the poor judgment I used. I think, if my head was a little more clear, I would've pursued my dreams," Marvin said as he looked down at his shoes as if to be disappointed in the calling up of past events. Adding in one last positive statement to reassure himself and me, a smile stretched across his face and he said confidently, "I will make something happen . . . someday. I think I just need to care a little more this time. One day the nowhere jobs I've taken will be a memory."

Listening to Marvin, I was aware he knew he made a mistake. He wished he had made himself into more than a 34-year old man who takes on unsuccessful jobs. Marvin taught me, in one hour, something that could affect my whole life. He taught me to put effort toward what I want and not give up. This interview will always let me remember to always try my best to succeed. I know Marvin feels his job and his knowledge don't really benefit anyone, but it certainly benefited me.

Nathalie Gage :: Grade 7
Annunciation School :: Minneapolis

THE THRILLING SPECTACLE

Through the years
Over the course of history
Around global hemispheres
Three blind mice
Three musketeers
Living on a lighted stage
Approaching the unreal
For those who think and feel

All the world's a stage

A show of hands, I raise mine high
Just as I
Would bow to kings
Long ago, before their farewell
A thousand, a million, a multitude of fans
Screaming, dreaming, shifting, drifting
"Rush—Live in concert"
The universal dream

Inhuman-like speed and precision
Knowledge second to Einstein
Spinning web like a spider
Like a spider crawling on your skin
Pounding on your temples
A surge of adrenaline
Every muscle tense to fence
The excitement within
The spirit of radio ever lingers
I cannot express in words "The Thrilling Spectacle"
The heart and mind united
In a single, perfect sphere

Time, stand still
Freeze the moment a little bit longer
Make each sensation a little bit stronger

Grace under pressure—Presto
Trick of light, moving picture
The superconductors turn the page
Pace the rage, light the stage
It's a craze
A permanent wave

Rush
"That's Entertainment!"

Ryan Linder :: Grade 11
Battle Lake High School :: Battle Lake

My Name's Rescue

K, thick tree, part of a butterfly wing. My name
traveled to a paradise island and fell asleep under
a grove of trees while a rainbow hovered above.
I, a fireman's pole. My name didn't wake
until the moon had risen. My name went to
look for food and fell asleep under a blackberry bush.
M, two high round hills. My name woke up to search
for some bananas when it noticed that the boat that
it came with was gone.
B, prescription sunglasses. My name paced up and down
the beach looking for the boat when my name fell in a very
deep pit that was covered by palm tree leaves.
E, bangs. My name was captured by two mountain
lions and dragged to a dry cave where he was told to wait for
the king of the mountain lions.
R like a gray flower falling apart. My name had to wait
for many days to see the king because there
were many names waiting to see the king.
L, a small part of a skyscraper. My name finally
saw the king and he wasn't a mountain lion
but my long lost brother!
Y, a toilet plunger. My name was set free by his
royal brother and remained with his brother and
became a king as soon as he learned the
mountain lion language.

Kim Donohoo :: Grade 5
Lino Lakes Elementary School :: Lino Lakes

"I am a Jew," was the first thing that David Levkovich told me during our interview, as if, perhaps, this was the best way to start out talking; for this one heritage, this one trait, was a key part, not in a religious sense, but in a persecuted sense, of his life. After this, he took the initiative, and asked me my grade and age. This was, as he remarked, to help him to know at which level he should speak to me. Once this was established, David began to speak. He did not need any prompting, for he had a story to tell, and tell it he would. It went something like this: He was born in Byelorussia, the capital of which is Minsk (he specifically told me this, out of pride and out of loyalty), as the son of two Jewish parents. His mother, an English teacher, taught British English in a local school. This aided greatly in our communicating, for he speaks English better than some Americans do; however, he did have a rather limited vocabulary, which made some of his deep thoughts and feelings hard to communicate, for lack of strong enough words. (Although I personally think that some of the things he told me could never be translated and understood with words in *any* language.) These feelings were ones of loyalty to a country who was unloyal to him, of unjustice to a man who himself was trying to be fair, and of torment, persecution and oppression to one that only wanted love, honor and courage to abound.

For instance, when he was fourteen years of age he heard his teacher lie. It wasn't a common ordinary lie that we all tell every day, but instead, it was a lie worse than all lies ever told, it was a falsity that contained the tainted information that Russian people were brought up with, and it was this information that would also, ultimately, lead to many people's downfall. You see, the teacher had told the students a part of the history of their motherland, only it was a new and improved history, the type that tells of the marvelous things that the premiers did, but never really did, and of the lovely and happy life that even the most common and most ordinary people had in Russia, but if you were to tell the most common and most ordinary person in Russia this, they, I am sure, would laugh at your ignorance. Well, anyway, David's conscience would not allow these lies to continue without at least *trying* to find out the real truth. Therefore David asked questions, such as, "Why do you tell us that our country has never made mistakes, that our government always acts on our behalf, and that because some people are different from others that they should be persecuted?" The teachers that had to answer David, as I gathered from my interview, did one of three things: They either didn't answer at all, they lied again, or they told his mother who, if you recall, was a teacher at his school, to, quite frankly, shut her son's big mouth up. However, David's exact words to me regarding the issue at hand were, "She was told to tell me not to ask so many questions." The rest of the message was left for me to figure out on my own, which I have done on this piece of paper.

Jim Fiebelkorn :: Grade 8
Hopkins North Junior High School :: Hopkins

SECRETS

A secret is like a bucket of water
if it spills out, it runs all over.

A secret is like a practical joke
if you tell it, you might embarrass the person.

A secret is like hanging on to a bar far above,
because if you let go of either the bar or the secret
you are in trouble.

A secret is like a sneeze
you try hard not to let it out
but it doesn't always work.

A secret is like an envelope
you can seal your
lips and not tell anyone.

Greg Duellman :: Grade 9
Worthington Area Junior High School :: Worthington

Back in Time!!!

THIS IS DEDICATED
TO
MRS. LORRAINE ROSAUER
who made this story possible!

Hi, I'm Michelle Towle. The year is 1938. I'm in my cozy, red farmhouse in Little Canada, Minnesota.

This morning I woke up at sunrise. It was so cold! The wind was creeping up the walls like eery spiders. A speck of dust withered by me and struggled over to the window frames. The sun was peeking over the fields of grain and wheat. Its rays danced around merrily and shone on my face.

I slithered my way out of the feather bed and heavy quilts. It is so uncomfortable sleeping on a feather bed! I'll toss and turn all night and wake up to cramps all over my body!

When I finally got the courage to get up, I went outside to the outhouse, where it's freezing! The outhouse is a very small, crowded, wooden shed, with barely enough room for one person!

Even though I was in there for only a few minutes, I hurried up very fast, because my toes were beginning to numb, my nose and cheeks were rosy red, and I had goosebumps all over my skin!

When I was out of the outhouse, I went into the chicken coop. In here, there are hundreds of chickens and chickadees rushing around everywhere, clucking, flapping and gawking about! It was just like a mad house!

I gathered all the fresh eggs and neatly placed them, one by one, into my baskets.

When I was finished doing this I went over to the barn, where I carefully milked the cows.

To milk a cow you place a large bucket or pail underneath the cow. Then you sit on a stool beside it. Next, you take hold of the udders, which look like big inflated gloves hanging down under the cow's stomach, and you pull on them one at a time to get the milk.

When I had gotten enough pails filled with milk, I very carefully brought the eggs into our house, being sure I did not drop or crack any; then I brought in the milk, being careful not to spill even a drop.

As I had been doing all this, my sister Anne had been setting six places at the table for breakfast and brought in the well water for washing and cleaning. My older brother Doug had slopped the pigs and collected firewood for the wooden stove, while my younger brother Phill had fed the animals and helped Doug with the firewood.

As my family and I ate our usual breakfast—oatmeal, scrambled eggs, fresh milk, and freshly squeezed orange juice—we quietly looked around our humble kitchen. It was very clean, with many homemade articles inside. Along our wooden stove were neatly carved cupboards made by Papa. Inside them were precious dishes passed down through our family from generation to generation.

After breakfast I put on my school clothes—a flower print dress sewn by Mama, a straw hat and my black button shoes. Then I quickly combed my curly brown hair.

Finally it was time to start for school. The walk to school is about one mile, and if we wanted to get there before the school bell rang, we had better hurry.

We started along the path to school and before home was out of sight we waved to Papa, who was out plowing in the fields with his team of horses, and to Mama, who was out in her garden weeding, tilling and picking ripe vegetables.

We now decided to take a short cut through the forest so we wouldn't be late for school. As we quietly walked through the forest we listened to the wind whispering to the trees, and the trees softly answer back by rustling their leaves. We listened to the birds chirping and flapping in the trees, and to fawns nibbling on fresh grass.

The grass was still slightly wet from the morning's dew.

To us they are just tiny drops of water, but to the ladybugs they are replenishing drinks.

We realized that we didn't have time to dawdle anymore — WE WERE GOING TO BE LATE FOR SCHOOL!!!

As we walked along more briskly we listened to the leaves crunch beneath our feet.

Finally we got to school. The bell had already rung, so we quickly went inside the school house. We were surprised and relieved to see that our teacher Miss Brown was not there yet.

We all sat down in empty seats while greeting our friends.

"Hi Tommy," I replied to 14 year old Tommy and his 8 year old brother Bill.

My best friend Louise came over to me and exclaimed, "Hi Michelle! How is your horse, Boots?"

"Hi Louise! Boots is dandy!"

I have my very own horse at home. She is a brown and white Palomino. I love to ride her! When I ride her, I like to gallop in the forest or on a path so I can enjoy all the sights, sounds, smells, animals, the breeze and my horse all at the same time.

Finally Miss Brown walked in.

"I'm so sorry I'm late, children. My mother just caught a cold and I had to bring her to Dr. Orstergan."

Our school is a one-room schoolhouse. It has only one classroom. In our classroom there are only eight children in it, all different ages.

Miss Brown goes around the classroom first teaching one grade, then another, then another, etc. As she goes from one grade to another, the grades that aren't being taught are able to work on their assignments or art.

Inside the classroom are eight desks that are lined up neatly in front of Miss Brown's bigger desk. There is a chalkboard on one side of the room and coat hangers on the other side.

From the outside, our school is a small red-brick building with a few windows and a black shingled rooftop.

The playground has one set of swings, one slide and two

bars to hang on. Most of the girls either swing or stay on the sidewalk and play jumprope, jacks, hopscotch, etc. The boys usually play tag, king of the mountain, slide down the slides, go on the monkey bars, etc.

After all of our assignments were given, and the chalk-board had been cleared, the school bell finally rang — SCHOOL'S OUT!!! Everyone rushed out of the schoolhouse.

We walked home with our friends, and on our way we dallied along in no particular hurry.

The girls all talked about school, parents, dolls, etc., while the boys talked about sling-shots, frogs, teachers, etc.

The walk home seemed so much shorter than the walk to school, because we were having so much fun. As we neared the top of a hill, we said good-bye to our friends, and continued on home. Before we knew it, we were passing Papa's fields and Mama's garden. Soon we were home!

When we got home Papa told us to put on our work clothes and come out and help him. So we all put on our shirts and overalls and went outside to help Papa. We helped Papa un-load the buck-board wagon, which still had flour from the grist mill and some nails, a hammer, a wrench, pliers and an axe left over from the hardware store.

After this we all went to round up the cows, pigs and chickens into the barnyard.

Now it was time for dinner. We all washed and cleaned ourselves while the water on the wooden stove gurgled to itself. Oh! That sweet aroma of smoked ham and fried bacon!! I couldn't wait to eat!

Soon dinner was ready, and so were we! We sat down, thanked God for our meal, and started eating.

During dinner Mama asked how we were doing in school.

"You kids had better be doing well in school. Do you real-ize Papa and I have to pay fifty cents a month for each of you to go to school?"

We ate the rest of dinner in silence, savoring each bite of our scrumptious meal: milk, smoked ham, fried bacon and broiled potatoes.

After dinner I took the hot water off the stove. We would use this water for washing dishes.

As Mama and I washed and dried dishes, I said to Mama, "There's this really dandy lipstick sample in my magazine that I'd like to send in for. I have my ten cents in stamps. Would you please send in my stamps tomorrow so I'll get the lipstick before we go over to Uncle Ben's house for New Year's Eve?"

"I'll send them out tomorrow on my way over to Grandma Clara's house."

"Thanks Mama! I'm sure you'll like the lipstick as much as I do."

It was getting very late now, and when I looked out the kitchen window, I saw the sun sinking beneath the trees, and one by one, the stars popped out joyfully.

It was about time to hit the sack, so we all rolled out our featherbeds and put on our night clothes. Then the boys helped Papa stoke and bank the fire. Anne and I helped Mama dust and sweep.

Now everyone cuddled up under their quilts and lay on their featherbeds just thinking. The kerosene lamps were turned off and everyone shut their eyes.

"Goodnight Mama and Papa."

"Goodnight Phill."

"Goodnight Doug."

"Goodnight Anne."

*SPECIAL THANKS TO MRS. ROSAUER WHO TOOK ME BACK IN TIME, SO THAT I WAS ABLE TO WRITE THIS STORY!

Michelle Towle :: Grade 6
St. John's Elementary School :: Little Canada

THE BALLET DANCER

She is a feather
floating in the sky.
She is the wind
that gives the earth motion.
She is the sun
dancing in the sky.
She is the nature we see.
She is the diamonds in the stars.
She is the lonely flower
drifting away.
She is the spark to the fire.
She is the kindness
in every human.
She is the animals
playing in the forest.
She is the person I will
always dream of being.

Teresa Berger :: Grade 6
Crestview Elementary School :: Cottage Grove

Symbol of Hope

Symbol of Hope

Before I came,
children had no hopes.
Before I came,
children had no imagination.
As I awoke,
a rainbow appeared.
The rainbow cast many colors on me.
It gave a horn to my forehead.
It gave many colors to my mane and tail.
After I came,
children began to dream,
After I came.
children began to imagine.
I was magic,
I was hope,
I was the first unicorn.

Denise Olson :: Grade 6
Columbia Heights Central Middle School :: Columbia Heights

Hope Poem

Sometimes when I'm lonely at
the beach with the sunset
it reminds me of a friend who
shared her love with me.
We talk to each other in our
hearts. The sunset helps pass
it on, we both hope we'll see
each other again and never
lose each other. Hope is the
one who helps me live.

Lirit Biton :: Grade 3
Highland Park Elementary School :: St. Paul

SELF PORTRAIT

Picture an aluminum
sculpture of man,
who looks like he's been sitting
for thousands of years.
He is grey, in a corner
where nobody looks,
only once in awhile,
when they say
how terrible he looks.
His head hangs down,
but on the inside he waits
and waits for somebody
to come along and look
and say, "Look
at that neat sculpture."
His inside is still
a light pink of hope,
but what's to hope for any more?

Darren Stevens :: Grade 5
Alice Smith Elementary School :: Hopkins

THE REDWOOD FOREST

This beautiful place is the cornerstone
of my mother's
and father's marriage.
I look around and see a tall
wondrous tree that stands high
above the clouds.
That tree would take me away from the
crowded streets of San Fransisco to a place of
pure peace running through each person
like a waterfall flowing down a hill.

Justin Kowalski :: Grade 3
Highland Park Elementary School :: St. Paul

The Man I Never Met

Through the years I have not
known who dad is.
as well as you did not know I.
We went around only with a smile,
no words were able to be made.
My fear was too strong to get to
know the man I never met.
WAIT!
Did you hear the crash?
I heard it too.
The glass shattered through the
hall.
I took a stone and threw it from
my side, as you did yours.
The glass wall is falling from
between us,
more and more each time the sun
arises.
I love dad, the part I know
and I know I will love the part
of dad that is still behind the
broken glass.
I am willing to throw all the
stones in the world and sweep up
the sharp clear pieces,
step across the line and say
HELLO.
HOW ARE YOU? MY NAME IS
KAREN, WHAT'S YOURS?

I LOVE YOU!

Charyn Daniel :: Grade 12
Alternative Learning Center :: St. Paul Park

To a Friend

I am a dark big sky,
    and you are the sun that lights me up.
I am the keys on the piano,
    and you are the music I play.
I am the grass that is brown,
    and you are the rain that makes my grass green.
I am a tree bare in winter,
    and you are the summer that puts leaves on me.

Michelle Jungers :: Grade 2
Centennial Elementary School :: Richfield

WHAT I THINK

When I write a poem,
my mind is like a big balloon
filled with feelings.
I wonder if I will be the same
writing a poem.
A thought pops into my head,
and I think
should I write it down or not?
Suddenly my pen lets it go.
The balloon has popped.
I am in the fresh clean air.
I am free.

Anita McKeown :: Grade 5
Callaway Elementary School :: Callaway

WATER

The water is my link to imagination.
The waves wash up the old and recycle
it to new. I follow the stream to the
world of facts. Where numbers and
letters scramble to enter my imagina-
tion to find new life. I see the heat
of the day in the cool water. The sun's
energy charges my mind until it swells
with pain. My head bursts open into the
water to renew itself back to peace
of mind.

Eric Stjern :: Grade 7
Fred Moore Junior High School :: Anoka

UNTITLED

I am the poet who sifts the nightmares
from the crevices in your minds, and leaves your
dreams filled with serenity.
I am the poet who seizes the venomous
snake before it slithers into the dark shadows
of the jungle in search of prey.
I am the poet who peers through a dense
mist into the delicate eyes of a child.

I express my thoughts through writing
and while I do, foes unite to form vast
walls of peace and love that overpower any
notions of combat.

My poetry reflects my innermost emotions
creating silky waves of understanding, as fragments
of my own enchanted kingdom are revealed
with hopes of others inspired to establish
their own.

Lisa Jacobson :: Grade 7
Oltman Junior High School :: St. Paul Park

(FROM A PLAY IN PROGRESS)

SCENE 4

TIME: DURING A PRAIRIE FIRE, LATE AFTERNOON

PLACE: THE KACY'S CORNFIELD

CHARACTERS: GRANDMOTHER KACY
HERBIE KACY
KATLINE KACY
CAL, a hired hand

(EACH CHARACTER HAS A SACK AND IS BEATING
OUT THE FLAMES. THEY OCCASIONALLY DIP THEIR
SACKS IN A TUB OF WATER)

CAL

Keep stomping, we've almost got it.

(LIGHTS DIM, COME UP ON *GRANDMOTHER KACY*.
SHE STARTS SINGING A CHURCH HYMN OF HOPE.
LIGHTS COME DOWN ON HER BUT SHE KEEPS SING-
ING. LIGHTS UP AGAIN ON *KATLINE* AND *HERBIE*)

HERBIE

(TO *KATLINE*) She's singing again, listen!

(THEY LISTEN)

KATLINE

It is beautiful! (LISTENS AGAIN, TRIES TO PICK UP THE
WORDS, SINGS A LITTLE OF THE CHORUS. *HERBIE*
COMES IN ON A FEW KEY WORDS)

(LIGHTS COME UP, ALL THE STOMPING STOPS)

CAL

The worst is gone but there's only a few plants left. We'll never get by. (SITS DOWN AND PUTS HEAD IN HANDS)

GRANDMOTHER

We did our best, Cal. We have a few seeds left don't we? (*CAL NODS HEAD*) We'll be all right. Our house is safe, so are the chickens, the horse and the cow. We can sell some of our garden vegetables if we have to.

CAL

We could get help from some neighbors who didn't get harmed.

GRANDMOTHER

We won't get any help from neighbors. We can get by just fine. (TO *KATLINE* AND *HERBIE*) Just like after your parents died. We did just fine, right?

HERBIE

It was hard for us, Grandmother. Katline became so upset. We should try to use some help.

(SOUNDTRACK OF GRANDMOTHER'S HYMN STARTS PLAYING, LIGHTS DIM, SPOT UP ON *KATLINE*)

KATLINE

It was the hardest thing for me to do, to say good bye to our parents before they died of smallpox. The last time I saw them they were weak, helpless and thin. The sitting and waiting for news while they lay there dying was awful. I couldn't sleep at night and I became pale and tired. When the news came that they had died, I couldn't stop crying. Who would care for us? What would happen? We didn't have enough money to hire a Reverend, it had been all spent for a doctor. So you, Grandmother, read from our bible. The thing I remember most then was not the suffering but the coffins being laid into the ground

and the dirt pile growing higher and higher on top of them.
(SHE STARTS CRYING. THE MEMORY MUSIC STOPS)

HERBIE
You remember it all? (SHE NODS) It was so long ago.

GRANDMOTHER
We got by without help then and we will now!

BLACK OUT

Cara Mia Bruncati :: Grade 8
Lake Country School :: Minneapolis

A River of Money

The dollar in my pocket
is like a green river
flowing through a forest
of enemy animals.
These animals fight over
the control of this river.
This river is dirty, old
and cold.

Without this river, these
animals will not be
civilized. There would
be no improvement and
no means of agreement.
This river is wise, clear
and warm.

No one knows where this
river begins, but all
they know is that it is
flowing by them.
Everyone wonders, Who
has seen this wonderful
river full of hatefulness
before me? Who will see
this river after me?
Who will see this river
after me?

This river is short, but long.
It depends on how much
water you have. This river
causes jealousy and causes hate.

Kelly Lamon :: Grade 9
Lanesboro School :: Lanesboro

"NO!! NO!!! GRANDPA! Don't Go!! NO!!!" Little
Marty's voice trailed off as his mother, a rather slim woman,
pulled him out of the stale, white hospital room where his close
grandfather, the only person that stood out in Marty's life, had
just lost contact with the world.

"Hush up Mart! This is a hospital. The sick people need
their rest! And I don't want you waking them up with your
awful crying. Now be quiet," said Mother as she had her iron-
tight grip on her son's upper arm.

Marty's face was as hot as a car door on a hot summer day
in August, but the rain-cold tears trickled off of his face like
snowflakes trickle out of the winter sky.

Mother seemed embarrassed by her son's encounter with
death. How was he supposed to react? Like an adult that only
deals with things after the sun sets, or like someone who thinks
nothing short of happiness when someone dies? For Marty, this
was his first real honest-to-life experience with death. He cried
and screamed for Grandpa. In hopes that he'd come back and
make everything perfect again. Mother's hazel brown eyes
scanned the hospital halls looking for anyone that seemed em-
barrassed or even the least bit annoyed by the fact that her son
was having a crying tantrum in the quiet stillness of hospital
halls. She was looking for an excuse to tell him to 'grow up and
act your age,' but she couldn't find one. Everyone else had their
own problems to deal with.

Marty crawled cautiously into the back seat of the family
car, parked in the visitor's lot in the front of the hospital. The
plush blue seats warmed his skin, for a short time only, from
the icy, cold world of death, but his ten year old mind couldn't
defrost. Grandpa was dead. He died while Marty was at the
window, looking out at nothing in particular. Mother was in
the hall, and Grandma was holding Grandpa's weak hand.

"I coulda saved him!" Marty shot out from the back. His
face was red hot, but a stark white. There was a well of tears
under his puffed eyes, making him look very queasy.

"Marty, we all must die. And there isn't anything you or any doctor can do to stop it." Mother tried her best to be comforting, but behind her shield of lipstick and mascara, she too felt as if something inside of her died and was gone forever.

"But Mom . . . I could have!!" More tears streamed down his cheeks even as he spoke. "If only I'd sent him a birthday card, or said 'thanks' for the baseball game, or gave him a hug this morning or—"

Mother cut him off. "Marty, he's dead. Gone. Now you have to get on with your life." Mother just kept her eyes on the unending road ahead of her. She then muttered under her breath, "I know I have."

"You don't understand!! He was MY Grandpa!!" Marty yelled, as if he was trying to fight a losing battle, but felt as if he could somehow win.

The conversation stopped then. The only sound heard was the murmuring hum of the car rolling humbly down the highway. Since nothing was being said, Mother flicked on the radio with a gentle punch of the small grey button in the right hand corner of the dashboard. The station was called K-F-U-N, and all it played was happy and uplifting tunes. At that moment the DJ played the Beach Boys hit 'Surfin' USA.' Mother had had enough "fun in the sun" to last her awhile from the first two verses. She then hit the number two button. Now, instead of happy music to lift Marty's spirits, Mother had flicked on the station of depressing classical music.

Everywhere he turned it was grey and dying. It wasn't fall or winter, but spring. The season of new lives. The day had started out with a warm, glowing sun to make everything good. Now it was almost afternoon, but the sun wasn't out. Some nasty rain clouds had moved in like an unwanted neighbor.

As Marty peered out his window he recognized the area. It would be another two to three hours before he was back home in the comfort of his own reassuring bedroom. Three long hours awaited him. He breathed in a deep breath of air. He felt a little better, but not much. He undid his seat belt and bent over and reached under the passenger's seat. He pulled out a fuzzy olive green blanket and put it on the seat next to him. He tightly bunched up his jacket and then locked both back doors. He put the jacket down on one of the arm rests, as a sort of pillow. He stretched out his knotted and tired legs and pulled the blanket up to his chin. He faced the seat and fell asleep. Leaving the horror of death behind him for the time being. Tomorrow. Tomorrow he could deal with it. Tomorrow.

Becky Comnick :: Grade 8
Mankato East Junior High School :: Mankato

TAKE ME OUT

Ten minutes left.
    Coach, take me out.
Seven minutes left.
    Coach, I've played the whole game.
    My body is dying a slow death.
    Bury me, please!
As I run down the field,
my legs are slowly disappearing.
The score is tied one-to-one.
    I cannot give up.
Our brutal opponents, only out
for blood, kick the ball out.
It is now in our hands,
our season, our fate.

In comes the throw, soaring
high in the gray sky, looking ever
so intimidating.
    Can I get to it? Will it be
    worth it? Will the nothingness
    below my waist get me there?
With my last spark of energy
I dive for the ball and belt it
with a limp, tired foot.
I hit the unforgiving ground,
not wanting to get up.
    Oh, I wish this was over! I
    don't care any more.
    So tired, so tired. It's got to be
    over by now.

The crowd reacts quickly
and begins to cheer.

The score, to my surprise, is no longer
one-to-one.
Two minutes left. Coach,
        don't you dare take me out.

James Steen :: Grade 10
White Bear Lake High School - North Campus :: White Bear Lake

To Grandma

I was a daisy, you were the wind,
but now that you left,
everything is calm and quiet,
there is no one around for me
to talk with or play with.
If you were still around
you would bring a breeze every day
to the meadow, but
you are not around,
and I am all still and quiet.
I will stay that way,
because you are not around
to bring the pleasant breeze
to the meadow that I grow in.

Jonathan Nagel :: Grade 4
Belle Plaine Elementary School :: Belle Plaine

THE HUNT

It was a cold day in late November as I headed into the woods hiking. I was at my grandpa's old farm by Baudette. It's in the middle of a large swamp about a hundred miles end to end. The howling wind gave me an uneasy feeling. I never did like that swamp much, but the forest was rich with rough grouse and deer and other things to watch. There were also timberwolves, one of the biggest wolves known to man. As I walked down the trail a grouse took flight, so away I went into the woods. About 200 yards in, I was stunned to see blood on the ground. I knew what it was right away. The wolves had killed a deer. I slowly swallowed and kept on going. Intrigued by what I might find, I moved further and further into the islands. I found five or six small pieces of the deer. Finally I came upon the carcass. It wasn't a pretty sight. There wasn't much left. I thought to myself, "You idiot! You are standing in the middle of nowhere; not another human in 90 miles."

I decided to start heading back because if the wolves were in a pack they would kill anything they could find. As I moved quickly through the woods, I caught a glimpse of a silvery white flash and I almost jumped out of my skin. I quickly jumped into the cane between two poplar islands and sat quietly. The wolf's nose started to twitch and I knew it smelled me. Then suddenly the wolf was gone. It was time for me to go. The pack would be back soon. As I started to run my heart skipped three beats when I heard the howling. In any other instance, it would not have bothered me so, but when the wolves howl during the day it can only mean one thing. The pack was gathering for the hunt and it also meant that I didn't have much time to get as far away as I could.

Dodging tree branches I ran frantically through the swamp. I decided to go into the cedar forest where it was easy going. Too bad the wolves thought the same thing, so I had no other alternative but to blaze a trail through to the grade (a small old logging road not in use for over 20 years). I ran hard, the brush cutting into my face, and the wolves not far behind. I had no gun to use, no knife to defend myself. So I had to move quickly, but I remembered I had some buck scent left over from deer hunting in my old jacket. I dumped it out on the ground to throw the wolves off my scent. I ran on but I was getting tired and had to stop and decided to climb into a cedar tree to spend the night.

In the morning I came out of the tree. Judging by my compass, I had to head east to the grade. I tried to run but my legs were too stiff, so I walked. Soon I came upon a beaver dam which backed up into a pond. I was getting a drink when I noticed him sitting on the other shore, less than 20 yards away: a large majestic lone wolf. I watched him for a second, sure to be quiet, but I stepped on a dry twig and he was gone. So was I. They'd be here soon. I still had a long way to go to get to the grade. I came to a part of the swamp that looked like you stepped off the face of the earth. As far as the eye could see was swamp grass and scrub brush. This was the worst place to be. This was a wolf haven because all the deer congregate here to eat red osier. There were at least three packs in that area. That was about 25 wolves. So I turned around and walked into the woods the other way. It had seemed like I had been walking for days but by my watch it had only been four hours. Finally I came across the grade. It seemed to go on forever so I ran quickly down it. I turned to see wolves right behind me—seven of them or more. I didn't stop to chat. All I could do was run!

I hit the edge of the field in a flat out run with seven wolves right on my tail. The cold wind cut through my clothes like a knife. Jumping the broken field fence, I started across the field. I ran tripping over the large clumps of mud and dirt. Suddenly I felt a wince of pain shoot up my leg. I looked down to see a large wolf hanging on me. So reaching down I started pulling all the hair off its face and beating on its head. It finally let go and I struggled to keep ground on him and the six others.

I came to the yard fence which wasn't going to stop them. As I went over one of them ripped off my shoe and tore a chunk from the sole of my foot. Limping with blood from the thigh down, I hobbled to the shed and peered into the gleaming hatchet on the wall. Grabbing it I hobbled back out into the cold, armed. The wolves were in the yard. Once again a wincing pain ran up my leg. This time I gave him a piece of my mind. With a screeching howl the wolf withdrew with half of his face missing. But there was one waiting to take his place. The hatchet fell once more and left a gash down the middle of the forehead of a larger wolf. In screaming howls of pain, he stumbled to the ground.

I didn't feel pity on the demons after looking at my legs covered in blood, theirs and mine. I finally came to the door of the cabin and opened it, looking in upon warmth, food and heaven.

The next day I went and knocked the teeth out of the two dead wolves and made a necklace. Then I hitched a ride to the hospital. And still to this day, five years later, I wear the necklace to remind me that good guys don't always finish last. My wounds have healed and in another 65 years, if things go right, I will be buried in that necklace made of the teeth that scarred me for life.

Chris LeClaire :: Grade 9
Bemidji Senior High School :: Bemidji

UNTITLED

My heart is a glowing sunset.
My lips are blades of steel.
My eyes are twinkling stars.
My mind is a golden link from a chain.
My voice is a warming song.
My bones are a frame of a house.
My skin is a piece of silk clothing.
My teeth are lakes and rivers shining in the sun.
My ears are two pistols shooting it out.
My blood is a golden arrow flowing.
My body is a harp playing melodies.

Josh Bruhn :: Grade 4
Kennedy Elementary School :: Hastings

Celebrate your cat. Celebrate
your dog.
Celebrate anything, just
celebrate along.
Celebrate your birthday.
Celebrate a song.
Just keep on celebrating, celebrating
along.
Celebrate good things.
Don't celebrate bad.
You celebrate when you win.
Celebrate when you lost.
Always do your best even
when they don't.
You can celebrate lots of things, but keep on celebrating.
Do, do, do.

Chris Mace :: Grade 4
Pine Hill Elementary School :: Cottage Grove

School Index

Program Writers 1989–1990

Sigrid Bergie
John Caddy
Nona Caspers
Bruce Cutler
Florence Chard Dacey
Kate Dayton
Norita Dittberner-Jax
Daniel Gabriel
Margot Fortunato Galt
Ellen Hawley
Dana Jensen
Jennifer Jesseph
Jane Katz
Judith Katz
Roseann Lloyd
Roy McBride
Ken Meter
Jaime Meyer
John Minczeski
Sheila O'Connor
Joe Paddock
Nancy Paddock
Alexs Pate
Stephen Peters
Ruth Roston
Mary Kay Rummel
Susan Marie Swanson
Linda Wing